INTRA-DAY TRADING STRATEGIES

PROVEN STEPS TO TRADING PROFITS

JEFF COOPER

Marketplace Books
Columbia, Maryland

ISBN: 1-59280-311-3
ISBN 13: 978-1-59280-311-8
Printed in the United States of America.

Table of Contents

INTRA-DAY TRADING STRATEGIES

FROM THE PUBLISHER

The editors at Marketplace Books have always kept a steady goal in mind, and that is to present actionable information on stock trading in the most straight-forward, practical medium available. Sometimes this involves a book, sometimes a newsletter, a DVD, or an online course program. What we've learned from the many products we've developed over the years is that a cross-medium approach is the most effective way to offer the greatest possible value to our readers.

So an idea was born. This innovative book and DVD set is one of the first in a series that combines a full course book derived from the actual presentation itself. Our idea grew out of a simple question. Students of stock trading spend a great deal of their own money attending lectures and trade shows. After all the travel, effort, and expense, that student will still have to assimilate a host of often complex theories and strategies. Sometimes he or she may want to ask a question or dig deeper into an issue, but they hold back—maybe because they still don't know enough about the bigger picture or maybe they don't even know some of the basic terminology. They may buy the DVD, but still…a lecture in itself is not a comprehensive learning tool and a person may still need yet another lecture or host of trial and error book purchases to master the subject.

So the question was: Does the average student of trading get enough out of an individual session to effectively carry their studies home and master a subject? The answer was a resounding no! Most attendees get bits and pieces of the message out of a long and expensive lineage of lectures, with critical details hopefully captured in page after page of scribbled notes. For those who are gifted with a photographic memory and vast organizational skills, the visual lecture is just fine, but for the rest of us, the combination of the written word and a visual demonstration is the golden ticket to the mastery of any subject.

A comprehensive approach to learning is the course you are about to embark upon. We've taken Jeff Cooper's original lecture and extracted his core content into an easy to read and understand course book. You'll be able to pour over every word of Cooper's groundbreaking presentation, taking in each important point in a step by step, layer by layer process. All of this is possible because our editors have developed this title in classic textbook form. We've organized and highlighted the key points, added case studies, glossaries, key terms, and even an index so you can go to the information you need when you need it most.

Let's face it, stock trading in any medium takes years to master. It takes time to be able to follow charts and pick out the indicators that mark the wins you'll need to succeed. And beyond the mathematical details and back-tested chart patterns, every presenter has three very basic premises for every student trader; they are to control your emotions, stay close to your trading plan, and do your homework. It's so important to know the full picture of the profession because it could either make you rich or put you in line for that second night job.

This DVD course book package is meant to give you all the visual and written reinforcement you need to study, memorize, document, and master your subject once and for all. We think this is a truly unique approach to realizing the full potential of our Traders' Library DVDs.

As always, we wish you the greatest success.

Meet Jeff Cooper

Jeff Cooper began his trading career in 1981 at Drexel Burnham working for his father, a hedge fund manager. Jeff left Drexel Burnham in 1986, choosing to trade exclusively for himself. After establishing a successful career as a private trader, he then went on to write three best selling books on the subject: *Hit & Run I*, *Hit & Run II*, and *The 5 Day Momentum Method*.

In addition to his books, Jeff has also released a DVD product, *Seven Set-ups that Consistently Make Money* where he teaches viewers exactly what it takes to earn a predictable profit in the trading arena. Jeff also has a new DVD charting course, *Unlocking the Profits of the New Swing Chart Method*.

Today, Jeff still trades for himself from his home overlooking the Pacific Ocean in Malibu California.

Introduction

Exactly What Is Intra-Day Trading?

"The trend is your friend." This is one of the oldest market maxims and one of the most profound.

It is also true, but, like a lot of maxims, it raises an important question: how do we define a "trend"? Most people would define a trend as a move of price in a specific direction. It is characterized by a series of higher high price levels, offset with swings to higher lows; or going in the opposite direction, a trend would be a series of lower lows with swings to lower highs. But I challenge you to ask a different question: What is the time frame of your trend? Are you referring to the trend existing weekly, monthly, or even hourly?

> **Time frame** is the window through which stock price trends are studied. A time frame may be daily, weekly, or monthly; it may also be hourly or consist of even smaller increments.

Determining Time Frames

One of the first steps every trader needs to determine is what time frame will be most appropriate to use. To a degree, this depends on the specific strategy you use. If you believe on one extreme that you are supposed to identify and buy quality growth stocks, and then hold them for many months or years, your time frame will be very long as well. If you are going to move in and out of stocks based on very short-term price swings, then the appropriate time frame must also be quite brief.

> **Growth stocks** are shares in a company whose earnings are projected to rise at a faster rate than that of the market. Dividends are typically not earned with growth stocks.

With the emphasis usually placed on price itself, the time frame is often overlooked by traders. I believe, though, that time is more important than price. A rapid price trend is different in significance than a very slow one covering the same price change, for example. In other words, rather than asking how many points a stock or index has moved, I want to know, "How long did it take?"

A monthly trend line gives us a broad view of the market, what the Dow Theory considers a primary trend. This can be significant based on how long one trend has been dominant, and how and when that trend turns and moves in the opposite direction. The Dow Theory is based on establishing primary trends and confirming them with a similar movement in a second index. So as far as long-term technical trends are concerned, the primary trend can serve as a highly significant one, both in terms of price and time.

> **Dow Theory** is a technical market theory observing primary trends only if and when a change in price movement is confirmed by a similar change in a second index. The theory was developed based on the writings of Charles Dow.

When we see a trend lasting two or three years, any change in direction gets our attention. I know that most investors become impatient if something doesn't change, especially when the market is bearish and you're long in stock. But putting impatience aside, you need to be able to step away from the preoccupation with long-term trends and look at what is happening right here and now. I agree with most technical analysts that a long-term (primary) trend is worth watching, if only to spot

> "But putting impatience aside, you need to be able to step away from the preoccupation with long-term trends and look at what is happening right here and now."

when it turns and begins going the other way. But I find it far more interesting and profitable to focus on a much shorter time frame.

> **Primary trend** is a major price direction in the broad market and is confirmed by movement in the same direction in a second index. The primary trend is usually the current long-term direction of the market.

Rather than looking at price trends from one month to the other or even from week to week, I think you can identify profit opportunities by simply being aware of some specific signals that occur day to day.

Intra-day Trading

This is where the topic of intra-day trading can be so useful. In my live presentations, I use the sub-title "Proven Steps to Short-term Trading Profits." And this is the key. With easy access through the Internet, cheap trading costs, and vast array of free and valuable charting tools, I—like many others—have come to the conclusion that the concept of long-term investing is dying, and that increasingly, people are going to invest in the future in terms of minutes and days rather than months and years.

> **Intra-day trading** is a technical system involving identification of signals and price behavior from one day to the next, anticipation of price movement based on breakouts and price gaps, and observation of likely movement based on changes between price levels from one day to the next.

Price behavior is what really counts and what determines whether you win or lose. Of course, time is more important than price, because price itself tells you little or nothing. For example, a particular stock or index might "rise" to the point that you make a 50% profit. But if that takes 10 years, your average annual returns is only 5%, and in my opinion, that isn't good enough. If the same index rises to the same level in six months, your annualized return is 100%, which of course is a much better outcome.

So as one of the most important precepts in intra-day trading, you need to recognize that time is more important than price because it is time that defines success. This is the first important fact to carry with you throughout this book.

> "Time is more important than price because it is time that defines success."

A second important fact to remember is that it is not the higher high prices or lower low prices that really matter, but what happens next. How does price behave after a sudden price shift, a breakout, or other unexpected change? This is what really helps the short-term trader to anticipate a change and to get positioned to maximize that change.

Breakout is a price movement above or below established high and low trading levels, which may signal subsequent behavior and enable a trader to anticipate the price direction.

Very few people talk about subsequent behavior. So much emphasis is placed on the trading pattern itself and on what it is supposed to reveal concerning strength or weakness of the stock, buyer, or seller interest in the price, or how what happened beforehand told you that the current pattern would occur. I say the past is done. Important and specific trading patterns are only interesting to the degree that they tell you something about the future. And when it comes to price movement, by the "future," I mean five minutes, the end of the current treading session, or the next day. Short-term. That's where the action is.

To the extent that you see price behavior react to a signal, there is very little actual analysis going on. You see a typical knee-jerk reaction by traders over one to three days, but after that you should be interested in seeing whether a new price direction is able to continue or not. What makes analysis so interesting is that all price change is a net difference between buyers and sellers, whose collective apprehension and competitiveness dictate just about everything in the short term. But know this, you can easily look through the short-term (one to three day) impulse and recognize the more permanent and stronger long-term trend. So on the one hand, you want to learn how to capitalize on short-term over-reaction among most buyers and sellers; and on the other hand, you want to be able to step back and recognize the larger, longer-term trend. You want to be able to see the slow and steady direction, while being able to profit from short-term chaos.

In this book I am going to summarize a few key principles in price movement and show you how to recognize when advantages or dangers are beginning to evolve. Price patterns can be very useful in timing your buy and sell decisions and, in fact, make all the difference in the world. Good timing can be profitable, and of course bad timing is disastrous on the same stocks. To cite another famous maxim, you should "Buy low and sell high." This may sound obvious, but in fact it is quite profound. Most investors do exactly the opposite because they have not mastered the art of recognizing signals. So they sell low to cut losses and buy high to get in on the trend; but, this trailing tendency is a mistake. I am hoping that the techniques and strategies I am going to show you will help you to overcome the "buy high and sell low" approach that is so common, and become a skilled short-term trader.

INTRA-DAY TRADING STRATEGIES

PROVEN STEPS TO TRADING PROFITS

Chapter 1

It's Like a Sword Fight Consisting of a Series of Pivots and Thrusts

Have you ever watched the sport of dueling? This is a very exact, precise sport involving posture, stance, and action. Pivots and thrusts. Pauses and turns. Action and reaction.

Price movement is similar in many ways. Upward and downward motion in price acts much like two duelers facing off and trying to dominate, make points, and come out ahead. And of course, timing is key. If your timing is good, you can make a profit. If it is poor, you can get a painful wound.

I sometimes find myself following a trend and thinking all is well and then changing my opinion. This is not arbitrary; my opinion changes because the character of price behavior changes. When I see a steady pattern evolve into an impulsive one, it becomes less predictable. But I want to get into some more detail about what I mean by "impulsive" price behavior.

The Wheels of Price and Time

I like to think about price and time not as isolated attributes of a stock or index but as part of the same thing. I refer to this as the "wheels of price and time," which work together like the precision movement inside a watch (figure 1.1).

FIGURE 1.1 - The Wheels of Price and Time

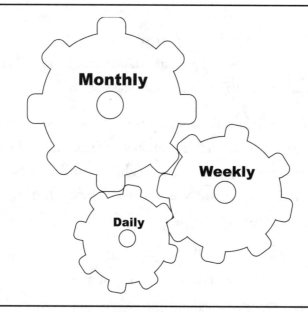

You have the big wheel (monthly) interacting with the smaller wheels, and that wheel's teeth lock into the trends you see on weekly and daily charts. This visualization of price and time help me to explain why I assign so much importance to a change in price behavior. Time frames work together just as the gears in a watch. The smaller time frames are fractals of the larger ones. You will see the same patterns repeating themselves over and over again, and I will show you examples of this as we move through the sections. The point to emphasize here is that if you think about trends as belonging in time frames, you can spot them more easily. You come to appreciate the fact that behavior in a very brief time frame has a context in a longer time frame, and its purpose is to fulfill the trend on both levels. The nature of price movement, like the duel between two experts, is to thrust, pause, and pivot back—in the case of price, the pivot goes back in the direction of the underlying trend if it is a legitimate movement.

Observing Market Behavior

If it helps to make this more vivid, we can try a different analogy. This is of the trend as a runner. When the runner inhales, it should provide momentum and enable the runner to continue forward. But if the runner is exhausted, he might simply collapse. The market is the same. When you identify a specific kind of movement, it enables you to take the temperature of the market and observe its behavior. Will price movement continue to move in the same direction, or will the trend collapse and fall apart? You can observe market behavior. Just as you can spot when a runner is about to collapse, you can also spot a weakening trend in the market. A runner's legs begin to wobble, he moves a bit from side to side, slows way down, and then his knees buckle. Think about this mental picture and then think about how stock prices rally and decline ... this is what I mean by observing behavior.

In my opinion, observing the behavior of prices as daily, weekly, monthly, or quarter charts turn up or down is the real sign of whether the bulls or the bears are in command. It's not the turn upward or downward that counts, and it's not the breakout or the breakdown. It is the behavior that happens next. A runner slows down and then collapses, or reinvigorates and sprints on a second wind. It is what happens next that matters.

Confirmation

The big question is: How do you get on board with a discovered change of direction? How do you discover enough information to act before you get confirmation from other related trends? This concept—confirmation—is so key to virtually all technical analysis that the question is a critical one. Once everyone recognizes a new trend, it's too late. You need to be able to act with extremely fast and immediate forms of confirmation, and that is where my intraday strategies come into play.

> **Confirmation** is the verification by a second indicator or pattern of what is implied about the direction or change in direction in price of a stock or index.

Once everyone realizes that a new trend is underway, it's too late to beat the averages, at least in the short term. Traditional methods of confirmation, such as movement in a second major index, usually take too long to use in the moment. Secondly, because trends start and end quickly in the short-term environment of the market, a trend is likely to be over and done with by the time the market at large realizes it.

In this situation—fast-moving, fast-acting—you need a method for efficiently and quickly recognizing emerging trends. You need to be on the train before it goes screaming out of the station; once you see the train passing by on its way, it is too late to jump on board.

> "Successful speculation is about anticipating the anticipators."

It is most interesting, in fact, that so many people are out there trying to get a jump on the market that their efforts can and do provide you with a real preview of what is about to occur. These traders attempting to get a jump on everyone are so plentiful that they create their own trend. This is good information. As legendary trader Bernard Baruch said, "Successful speculation is about anticipating the anticipators."

Shakeouts

So how do we get on-board before the trend has been confirmed, before a new trend has been confirmed, or at least a respite in the current trend? Once a move is confirmed for everybody to see, usually you get a shakeout. So maybe once we have seen a top or bottom signal, that means the market is ready for some change.

> A **shakeout** is a change in direction, usually temporary, in which prices are adjusted for consolidation at the bottom or profit-taking at the top.

The goal in intra-day trading is to identify specific patterns foreshadowing shakeouts or downright reversals in trends. You need to find a solid risk-to-reward point for entry into a stock or index. But that should be set to occur only after you see the signs of a cyclical bull or secular bear market. How do you get on board before the market shows its hand to everybody? How can we capitalize on price and direction change before the meat is already off the bone, so to speak?

> A **cyclical bull** is a market condition in which prices rise as part of a broad price and value cyclical phase within the broad economy or the market economy.

The market is perverse. In a bear or volatile market, when trends are overly choppy, recognizing tops and bottoms are very momentary, and trends can be extremely short-term in nature, lasting a day or less in some cases. In order to capitalize on the here and now, you are going to need efficient methods for timing your entry and exit. You need to play the short-term, because if you wait for long-term signals to develop, you'll only have history and a list of "things I should have done" instead of profits.

> A **secular bear** is a type of negative market condition that tends to be long-term in nature, often occurring during recessionary economic times.

Everything in the market is an act of faith, and this is the point. It's unpredictable, and price can move in any direction at any time. Strong and confirming signals are merely indicators, not sure things. If you become effective in using buy and sell set-up signals to time your decisions, your percentages will improve, but you will never get to 100%. The uncertainty of the market ensures that this can never occur; there are too many unknown influences, random events, and illogical forces at work to bring true order to the market's chaos. So if you want to wait until the market proves itself, you're going to be late for the party.

Chart Interpretation

The key to short-term trading is going to be found in pattern recognition on the daily chart. What is the daily chart doing? By observing a subtle change of character in price on a very small wheel of time, you can make a series of well-timed assumptions. If the daily chart is turning down, is the low going to occur immediately, or will the trend continue downward for an extended period of time?

Chart reading is easy, and any five-year-old can do that. If a stock's price is traveling from the lower left-hand corner to the upper right-hand corner, he's going to see that the stock is in an uptrend. Why can't we, as adults, believe what we see? I think the difference is psychology. We arrive in the trading arena with much baggage and many preconceptions. These have developed as a culmination of all our profits and losses in prior trades. We believe that logic and thinking are the keys to taking money out of the market. But in fact, no matter how much studying you do or time you put in, if your timing is off, you're going to lose. It's that simple.

Chart reading is easy. But chart interpretation requires greater skill. Otherwise, someone would have developed a system by now to accurately predict the market. But in spite of the dozens of claims to that end, it just can't be done. No computer program or trading system can interpret behavior as accurately as your own mind; and price movement is the net result of offsetting buyer and selling psychology at every instant.

> "This means that we have to trade based on what is, not what we think should be or want to be."

Here is the key lesson you need to remember about this: Speculation is observation, pure and experimental, like the mind of a five-year-old. Thinking isn't necessary and usually just gets in the way.

This means that we have to trade based on what is, not what we think should be or want to be. For example, I was watching CNBC one evening at a point when the market was falling over a period of time. One of the talking heads was being taken to task for being bullish throughout the fall. He explained, "Well, I've been wrong, but I've been wrong for the right reasons."

That's dangerous thinking. That's a recipe for disaster. That's just not how you make money in the stock market. The market is always right, except for two times, at the very bottom and at the very top. And of course, trying to pick the very bottom and the very top may be a lot more emotionally gratifying than trying to get on a trend; but, if you want to succeed in consistently taking trading profits, you have to decide whether you want to be right or you want to make money, and they are non-exclusive of each other. They have nothing to do with each other. It's necessary that you try to divorce and suspend your disbelief in what you see and just follow the price. Price is the final arbiter. In the next section, I expand on this to show you how price patterns reveal the trend, and how you can use those patterns to get a jump on price.

Self-test questions

1. The "wheels of price and time" is a reference to:

   a. The "turn" seen by insiders, a tendency for buyers and sellers to reverse roles at pivotal points in the trend.

   b. A likely outcome for cyclical movement, which invariably returns to its starting point.

   c. Behavior of the two elements, like the gears inside of a watch.

   d. Those key stocks that drove the market and cause trends.

2. Confirmation is:

   a. The ticket a trader receives advising that a trade has failed.

   b. The validation of a trend, found in a second indicator drawing the same conclusion about the direction of price.

   c. A large block trade by an institutional investor which confirms the good timing of a previous trade by an individual.

   d. Of interest only to highly technical study of the markets.

3. A shakeout is:

   a. Fear or panic setting in to the market after prices begin to fall, in which the most nervous investors sell everything at the worst possible time.
   b. A temporary adjustment in price, usually involving consolidation at the bottom or profit-taking at the top.
   c. The consequence to corporations when investors perceive that earnings trends have weakened, usually resulting in a lack of interest in the stock.
   d. Any news that adversely affects stock prices.

4. The key to understanding the short-term trend is found in:

   a. The 200-day moving average in convergence with the 20-day moving average.
   b. A detailed study of candlestick charts.
   c. The long-term chart and well-established trading patterns.
   d. Pattern recognition in the daily chart.

5. Speculation is simply a matter of observation. Thinking:

   a. Usually just gets in the way.
   b. Is the key to intelligent judgment every speculator needs.
   c. Enables you to recognize a false pattern and avoid it.
   d. Tells you specifically what to observe.

For answers, go to www.traderslibrary.com/TLEcorner

Chapter 2
The Truth About Indicators

You might ask yourself: How can I make money in the market even if I am intellectually bearish?

In other words, if your logical mind tells you that prices are going to go down, how can you profit in such a market? In fact, you can profit in both up and down markets, whether you play only short-term price swings or look at long-term indicators and play those. The old-style belief that investors only make money when markets go up is simply false.

The market is master. We cannot overlook this simple fact of life. Our job as traders is to recognize what the master tells us, and to then follow. It does not matter what we think; it only matters that we know how to recognize patterns and react to them. In my opinion, this 95% psychological market is not as complicated as some people make it. The market is an emotional, irrational animal and not a reasonable, thinking, logical being. If we must assign a conscious mind to the market, I would think of it as a bewildered beast.

The good news is, because we humans tend to think in images, the market does display visual representations of the emotions exhibited by most traders. Of course it is the collective emotional output of traders that breathes life into the market, and the truth about patterns is that they do represent those moods, trends, and emotions. The patterns are traced out and carved in the market daily, and charts tell us what the smart money is doing or, more reliably, what prices are about to do and where the smart money should be going right now.

> "So you need to remember that only three forces matter in the market: price, time, and pattern."

So you need to remember that only three forces matter in the market: price, time, and pattern. The pattern, of course, is merely a visual outcome of price and time. But I separate it and give it value because we have to rely so heavily on how price and time play out, and in how we see the price trends as they emerge.

I don't really use any indicators. Remember, all indicators are derived from price. Some are derived from a combination of price and volume, so they are of second degree magnitude. Why don't we just go right to the horse's mouth and deal with price itself? Price is the final arbiter. As I have said before, speculation is observation because no system exists that is superior to the human mind, which can synthesize experience and put these pieces of historical occurrences of these patterns in the proper context. And that's what it's all about, taking patterns as they exist and looking at the odds, creating an edge and seeing what they tell us historically, how they pan out.

The Right Mindset

I believe there is a reason that most traders do not realize profits consistently. They view the market as their adversary. They project all their fears and hopes onto the market and want to blame the market for everything that's going wrong, for the money they're losing, for all the bad things that are happening. But this is completely irrational.

The market is not an arena to work out personal issues of self-worth, or to figure out your feelings. There are many other arenas in life that are much cheaper to do that in. If you're looking for approval and self-worth, the market is the last place for that.

I'm going through these explanations because I want you to begin thinking in practical terms about the pattern you are going to use, about price and time, and about a pragmatic approach to trading. You need to be able to take small losses and pat yourself on the back when you do. The analogy of a baseball player explains this concept. Guys that are hitting .300 are getting struck out or aren't getting to base seven out of 10 times, but they're making millions of dollars a year. If they let the seven times that they didn't connect and put wood on the ball throw them off or rattle them, they wouldn't be making millions of dollars a year. That is very much like trading. You don't need to even be right 50 percent of the time. If you can accept taking small losses and wire your brain to that, you can make money at this game by just moving up your trailing stop.

> **Trailing stop** is a condition attached to a market order requiring a position be closed if and when a specific price is reached, often used to accept small losses rather than allowing them to decline into larger losses.

Momentum

A smart, defensive approach won't work if you see the market as an adversary. Winning each and every trade will become so important, based on anger rather than on logic, that you would prevent yourself from seeing the issues clearly. That's crucial because when the market subtly changes its behavior or does something it is not expected to do, that's when momentum sets in.

> **Momentum** is a tendency for a price direction to continue or to pick up speed when investors and traders fuel a trend after it has begun.

Momentum might be the most important indicator. And ironically, it isn't actually an indicator at all. But as a specific kind of trend, it's a key to revealing how to take profits out of the market.

An example of how this works: I remember 1994 as the worst bond year that we'd seen in decades. The stock market made a top in January of that year, then went down hard. From the first week of April, prices went sideways all the way until December, even though the bond market continued moving down. So the stock market went down in April and then went sideways for the rest of the year.

When the pressure of the bond market came off—and it was a horrible bear market in bonds—that was the beginning of the parabolic move up in stocks from 1995 up into 2000.

So stocks were talking. The way they held together in the face of the worst bond market of the century revealed the pressure cooker of that market. And you see this on all time scales. The most obvious one is when bad news comes out on a stock or when somebody downgrades it, and the stock bounces right back. Typically you may continue to see strong buying by institutions. They're not throwing out the baby with the bathwater because somebody at another firm downgrades it; they're using it as an opportunity to buy. You've got to try to put yourselves in their shoes and their mindset when you see that happen.

So when you see the market putting its money where its mouth is and you see bad news shrugged off by the market, that's what generates momentum. This, as traders, is what we all should be seeking. That's when you find the sweet spot. And that's when we all think we're geniuses until Mr. Market decides to teach us who's boss again.

Pattern Interpretation

Let's take a look at some specific charts so that I can show you how these concepts come to life. I have given you my philosophy about the market; now let me show you some examples of how patterns can be interpreted.

The first chart is a summary of the S&P 500 Index (figure 2.1). On March 12, you see a low and, based on the previous movement in this stock, it's a clear buy signal. This is an example of a lizard signal. That's the case because the price reached a new 10-day low,

FIGURE 2.1 - **S&P 500 Index (CBOE) - Daily**

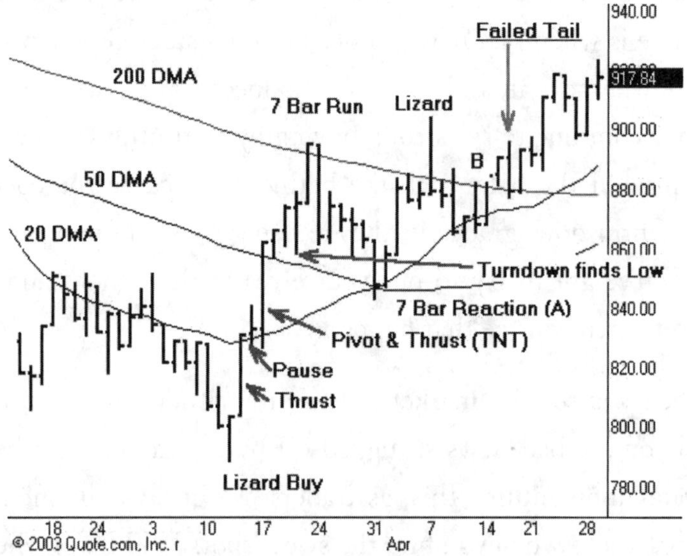

Februaru 12, 2003 thru April 29, 2003
For larger view, go to www.traderslibrary.com/TLEcorner

while it opened and closed in the top 25% of the bar. This is called a lizard because of the unusual pattern and because price invariably snaps right back the following day. On the opposite side is a sell lizard. This occurs when the price reaches a new 10-day high and the opening and closing prices occur in the bottom 25% of the bar.

> **Lizard signal** is a chart pattern involving a 10-day high or low and placement of opening and closing price. A lizard buy occurs at a 10-day low and when the stock opens and closes in the top 25% of the chart; a lizard sell occurs at a 10-day high and when the stock opens and closes in the bottom 25% of the chart.

The nature of price movement is to thrust, pause, and pivot back in the direction of the underlying impulse. When this occurs, it is a sign of genuine momentum. I refer to this as a TNT movement in price. It is typified by thrust and turndown, and figure 2.1 provides an excellent example of this tendency in a price pattern.

> **TNT movement** is the tendency of price movement in periods of momentum, to thrust and turn. The direction may be thrust upward and turn downward, or the opposite.

The lizard buy is followed by a classic sign of upward momentum. Note the very strong upward thrust, then a pause, then a pivot and thrust (TNT) returning to the upside, which is the underlying direction and momentum in this price pattern. The first thrust is especially strong and you will note that the day closed at the top of the day's range. This is a good example of how you observe price behavior. The trend line and stock action are not simply a matter of price from day to day; it also involves the pattern and where a stock opens or closes within its daily trading range.

Seven-bar Trend and Seven-bar Reaction

There is a certain symmetry to some price movements as well, and by observing these you will be able to recognize and even predict how price movement is going to occur in a short-term trend. From the first thrust day, a seven-bar trend occurs twice. First is a seven-bar run, demonstrating momentum in the upward direction. Second is a seven-bar reaction, or movement in the opposite direction.

> **Seven-bar trend** is a trend in one direction lasting over seven periods. These involve runs (the movement in an underlying direction) and reactions (offsetting price movement in the opposite direction).

The run and reaction demonstrate another important factor. A turndown in price (in this case, the reaction) is likely to find the low, that support level that helps you decide whether the momentum is real or only appears real. During periods of momentum, the important support and resistance levels are dynamic; so, whenever you can establish their levels with price patterns, it improves your ability to recognize when to enter or exit the position.

The seven-bar reaction in this instance is important because support occurs right at the necktie of two moving averages, the 20-

> **Reaction price movement** is a direction opposite that of an established trend.

period and 50-period. Also note that this support level happens to be the same as the previous high, seen at the beginning of this chart and before the lizard buy signal emerged.

> **Support and resistance** is the outer levels of a trading range. Support is at the bottom and resistance is at the top. These are the price levels where buyers and sellers currently operate and, outside of those levels, trading will not occur until the trading range evolves and changes.

Because the support level occurs at the necktie, and this price level coincides with a previous price high level, it forms a picture of a perfect pullback. It also demonstrates that the market tends to play out its short-term trends in groups of threes and sevens. The necktie ends a seven-period pullback.

> **Necktie** is a convergence point of two moving averages, so called because the lines move together and meet, then cross each other.

How do you act at this point? Realistically, we have a broad view of price both before and after the end of the seven-period reaction. But at that point, what action can you take? What does this pattern reveal? If we pretend we don't see the following price rise, how do we anticipate this kind of movement?

The reaction and necktie occurs without even a two-day consecutive low. The reaction merely falls to that point and then immediately moves back up. This is a sign of strength, telling you that the momentum is real. The reaction takes price down but it can't keep it down long enough to end the price momentum.

Following these developments we next see a lizard sell signal. Does this mean you should go short? No. There's no reason, based on the recent pattern and upward price strength. Remember, not all lizards are created equal. In this case, there's no follow-through or continuation to the downside. You see a failed test followed by strong return to the upside. This leads to what I call plus-one, minus-two. A plus-one is seen at the new three-day high, which began three days after the failed test. That test itself was a strong buy signal.

> **Compression move** is a price pattern and trend in which price remains below the 200-day moving average for 120 days or more.

Compression Move

The symmetry of the seven-bar reaction is part of the consolidation. But the downward move was a failure because it couldn't be sustained. At the same time you want to keep an eye on the all-important 200-day moving average. Note that as the strong upward momentum continues, the 200 is trending downward and crosses through the momentum itself. Eventually, the price will have to meet up with the 200 because that dictates longer-term price direction. But for now, we're concerned primarily with the short-term trend, meaning what happens over a few periods. This situation, which developed under the 200-day moving average, is called a compression move. This occurs when price remains below the 200 DMA for more than 120 days. So price moving through that average is not immediately disturbing; in fact, it is properly interpreted as a promising short-term signal.

> **Second mouse** is a second signal confirming a trend, so-called because it often occurs that the first mouse sets off a trap, and the second mouse gets the cheese.

A lot of bears would want to assume downward movement the first time price tagged the 200, which you see just before the seven-bar reaction. I recommend that you not react to this first tag, but at the lizard; and sure enough, that was followed by a three-day decline. I like to call this the second mouse because typically the first mouse gets trapped and the second mouse gets the cheese.

Self-test questions

1. There are only three forces at work in the market. These are:

   a. Buyers, sellers, and economic change.

   b. Institutions, retail investors, and regulators.

   c. Uptrends, downtrends, and consolidation.

   d. Price, time, and pattern.

2. A trailing stop is a condition attached to an order:

   a. Requiring that further buys must stop when margin limits are reached.

   b. Requiring that positions be closed if and when a specified price level has been reached.

   c. Automatically establishing a program of dollar cost averaging.

   d. Only when the brokerage firm needs to limit exposure to excessive trading activity in an account, usually of a day trader.

3. Momentum is:

   a. A condition in which a price direction is continued by the increased activity of investors, fueling the trend.
   b. A sign of panic in the market, caused when many investors sell at the same time in response to a false rumor.
   c. The tendency for retail investors to imitate the trading activity of large institutional investors.
   d. Accomplished when a corporation eliminates its competitors and dominates its industry.

4. A lizard signal:

   a. Is a slow-moving trend that slows down and then stops.
   b. Describes a trend moving in a single direction indefinitely, caused by momentum.
   c. Is one with a specific bowl-shaped pattern, identified by well-known technician Charles P. Lizard.
   d. Involves a 10-day high or low price level, coupled with both opening and closing prices occurring in the top or bottom 25% of the day's trading range.

5. Support and resistance is:

   a. The defined borders of a trading range, with support at the bottom and resistance at the top.

   b. Any trading occurring outside of the established trading range, following a volatile and high-volume period in which the range's limits are tested..

   c. A name given to stock prices when buyers dominate conditions, so called because in order to support side a move, seller resistance must be overcome.

   d. The degree to which speculators respond to an IPO, either supporting the new public issue, or resisting the unknown entry to the market.

For answers, go to www.traderslibrary.com/TLEcorner

Chapter 3

The Simple Tools are Often the Best

The whole idea of chart analysis is thought to be complicated. But if it is done right, the whole process can and should be quite simple.

Let's take a look at a chart that demonstrates what I'm talking about: trend line behavior on a weekly pattern. One of the keys to success in the market is trying to keep it simple. It sounds very trite, but there's so much out there with computer modeling and complicated and detailed plans that don't really give you much insight at all. It can be very overwhelming.

In order to see something happen in the market, you have to place it on your radar. You can't be greedy. You have to be able to drill down and look at only a few things if you're ever going to take any money out of the market. And by that I mean that some of the simplest tools, such as the straight trend line, are the best.

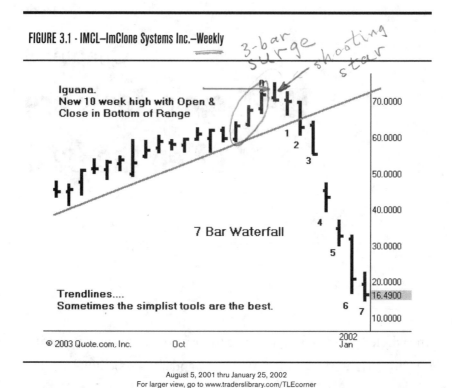

FIGURE 3.1 - IMCL–ImClone Systems Inc.–Weekly

3-bar surge

shooting star

Iguana.
New 10 week high with Open &
Close in Bottom of Range

70.0000

60.0000

50.0000

40.0000

1

2

3

7 Bar Waterfall

4

5

30.0000

20.0000

16.4900

Trendlines....
Sometimes the simplist tools are the best.

6 7

10.0000

© 2003 Quote.com, Inc.   Oct

2002
Jan

August 5, 2001 thru January 25, 2002
For larger view, go to www.traderslibrary.com/TLEcorner

Let's look at a weekly chart of ImClone (figure 3.1). Notice that for this stock, after every turndown on the weekly chart, you never see any follow-through. You didn't necessarily see a thrust up, but this reveals that the trend was still up even on a down day. Every time the weekly chart turned down, you still found the low, and then it stopped. Then you see the turn. It was clearly signaled. Note that right before the turn downward, there were three days of progressively higher high price levels, offset by progressively higher lows. I call this a three-bar surge because the signal follows the established direction but also provides an exceptionally strong warning that the trend is about to end. The same thing works on a downtrend. You know you're reaching the bottom when you see a three-bar surge with consecutive lower lows offset by lower highs.

> **Three-bar surge** is a strong signal that the current trend is coming to an end. It consists of three consecutive bars with higher highs offset by higher lows; or on the downside, by lower lows offset by lower highs.

The implication of the three-bar surge is that it is time to get out of a long position or to go short. But are you sure the trend is ending? In this example, it is actually confirmed strongly with a lizard—a new 10-week high with both opening and closing prices in the bottom 25% of the trading range. Because this lizard appears on a weekly chart rather than a daily, I have made the distinction by naming it the iguana (because it's a larger chart).

> **Iguana** is a lizard formation appearing on a weekly chart.

Remember, the market plays out in patterns of threes and sevens. You see this in the first hour of a 10-minute search bar, for example. In figure 3.1, you see a three-bar surge into the high. Now look at what happened after the three-bar surge and confirmation from the iguana: The price began falling. And there you see immediate confirmation of a change in the trend: A three-bar surge to the downside (progressively lower lows offset by lower highs) followed by a breakaway gap. That is a gap in which you also expect to see high volume and a strong trend.

A **breakaway gap** is a type of gap involving high volume and occurring as part of a very strong trend, often seen at the beginning of a reversal.

If those people in a long position did not get out at this point, they were in trouble. Although they should have sold quickly as soon as the three-bar surge was confirmed by the iguana, there are always some people left even after all of those red flags. So if you were still long after the breakaway gap, it was time to cut your losses. In this case, it is wise to remember the maxim, "Your first loss is your best loss."

Referring back to the argument about what a three-day surge means, you could argue that the downward surge marked 1-2-3 should have worked as a buy set-up. But a couple of things have to come into play here. First, instead of confirming the buy signal with some other signal such as a lizard, a narrow range day with high volume, or a brief period of consolidation, the stock went into a gap and then a big freefall. The second thing was external to the chart, and this is where you just have no control over what price is going to do.

Remember, price can do anything at any time. The signals and patterns we use only imply what is likely to occur. In this case, the weekly period around January, 2002, you will recall that in late December, 2001, ImClone had just gotten bad news from the FDA and had some high-level insider trading going on as well. So this strong downward turn was caused more by those factors than by any chart-specific patterns. It is always that way. Without any special external news or developments, price patterns are likely to emerge "normally," but a sudden event affects everything. The strong uptrend here probably anticipated FDA approval and, of course, when that didn't happen, the price went south. Then the trend was aggravated by the sale of shares by insiders.

This downward cascade in price, noted by numbers 1 through 7, falls once again into the theme of price moving in threes and sevens. Some analysts give names to this phenomenon. W. D. Gann wrote that seven was the number of panic.

Let's look at another example of this mathematical consistency.

The daily chart for Coach Inc. (COH) shows you what I mean by a series of threes (figure 3.2). You often see this three-part action in straight uptrend or downtrend patterns or, as in this case, typified as a plus-one, minus-two pattern. Here you see a small gap followed by a price thrust (+1) and then a two-period pullback (-2). This sets up a great risk to reward opportunity. The following morning, you see price continue to surge upward. The pattern of three sets this up. You see this even more clearly on an hourly chart of the set-up (figure 3.3).

In this kind of situation, I am basically a day trader, meaning my orientation is toward fast in-and-out trading in a stock. Or, more accurately, I may act as a swing trader, meaning I want to be in the stock no more than a few days and trade on the very short-term price swings you see in a two- to five-day period. When I print out my daily charts, I typically want to look back 10 to 30 days. For hourly charts, I'll go back a week, and for 10-minute charts, I want to see five to seven trading days. So the increments of the charts are going to dictate how much history I need to understand the current trend. In the Coach Inc. example, there's a pattern you will see over and over again. Think in terms of tests. The market likes to break out and pull back as a series of tests. When these tests occur, they are frequently followed by what I call a "one, two, three swing." This is not a pullback in the sense of consecutive highs or lows on the bars; it is, in comparison, a series of

FIGURE 3.2 - COH–Coach Inc.–Daily

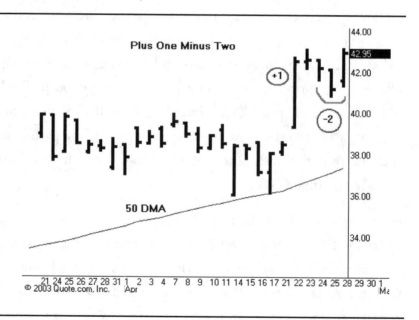

March 21, 2003 thru April 28, 2003
For larger view, go to www.traderslibrary.com/TLEcorner

test swings. This chart starts out with just such a test and, of course, the test sets up an opportunity.

A **day trader** is an individual who buys and sells positions in stock within a single trading period, usually ending the day with no open positions.

So in this case the 1-2-3 swing takes price up and then sets up a series of falling prices (also note the triple bottom, another example of something happening in threes). When you compare daily and

FIGURE 3.3- COH–Coach Inc.–Hourly.

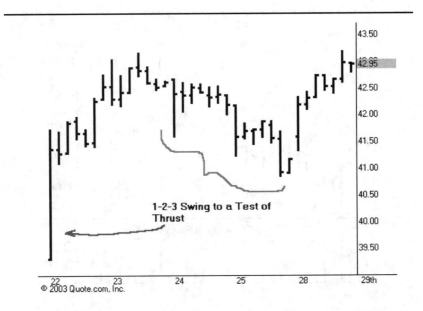

1-2-3 Swing to a Test of Thrust

April 22, 2003 thru April 28, 2003

> A **swing trader** is anyone who moves in and out of positions in a short-term time frame, usually two to five days.

hourly charts as in this example, you will often be better able to get into the sweet spot to improve your timing. I want to show you yet another example of the same thing, a three-part pattern.

This shows, in a daily chart, a plus-one, minus-two formation (figure 3.4). What is interesting here is that you also see the response to the set-up immediately, and we live in a universe where immedi-

FIGURE 3.4 - AVID—Avid Technology Inc.—Daily

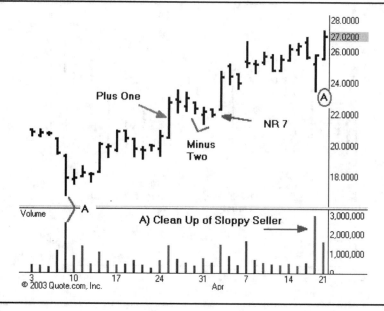

March 23, 2003 thru April 21, 2003
For larger view, go to www.traderslibrary.com/TLEcorner

ate gratification does not always arrive so easily. I have also noted on this chart the narrow range, marked NR7, because it has the narrowest range out of the previous seven-day periods (starting at the plus-one point). This foreshadows the following set-up that follows and consists of a series of three-part patterns.

> **Narrow range** is a period, usually a day, having a narrow gap between opening and closing prices, and with little or no trading occurring above or below those levels; a NR 7 day is one whose trading range is the narrowest of the previous seven days.

This narrow range seven (NR7), where you see a brief gap-and-go formation, is additional confirmation and yet another clue about what is taking place. Note the spike in volume at the bottom of the chart taking place at the same time at the range expansion at A. It is fairly obvious that this volume and price decline was simply a seller wanting to get out because you will also note that the price finished the day higher. So I call this a clean up of a sloppy seller, someone who was not reading the chart accurately and who overreacted to the prior day's lower close without a clear chart-based reason.

You get even more insight on this kind of formation when you look at Avid Technology's 10-minute chart. In this case, the day begins with an exceptionally strong 3 bar plus surge, and from that point forward, the price remains in an extremely narrow trading range.

This shows you a good example of a pattern you will see a lot in the first hour (figure 3.5). I call this amateur hour because so many traders are moving in and out of positions without really know-

FIGURE 3.5 - AVID–Avid Technology Inc.–10 minute

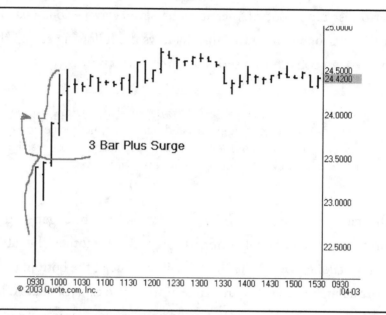

3 Bar Plus Surge

© 2003 Quote.com, Inc.

April 2, 2003
For larger view, go to www.traderslibrary.com/TLEcorner

ing why. But knowing this presents a great opportunity for the observant trader. You are often able to make a fast profit on either the long or short side by being aware that the first hour of trading is often going to exhibit this kind of pattern. But if we look at another daily chart for Avid, we see something else going on as well, and in this instance, watching the 50-day moving average is instructive (figure 3.6).

What was probably going on here was continuing confidence by institutions, causing other institutions and retail investors to climb

FIGURE 3.6 - AVID—Avid Technology Inc.—Daily Chart 2

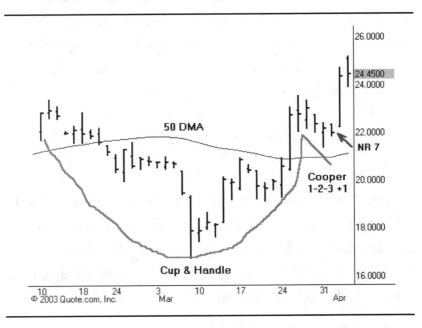

50 DMA

NR 7

Cooper
1-2-3 +1

Cup & Handle

26.0000

24.4500
24.0000

22.0000

20.0000

18.0000

16.0000

10   18   24   3   10   17   24   31
© 2003 Quote.com, Inc.   Mar   Apr

March 10, 2003 – April 1, 2003

on board. Some of these trends are self-fulfilling but brief. Here you see that many investors were buying shares all the way up the trend. But at the same time, note how the 50 DMA is moving in on the price.

This pattern involves a well-known formation called the cup and handle, which I have marked on the chart. It involves a rather predictable downward motion, a bottom, and a return to the upside in a cup-shaped pattern.

When you see a strong price decline such as the one at the beginning of March in figure 3.6, you know that it grew out of the consolidation period. This pattern often means that an institution has broken the stock through sales, perhaps in an attempt to create bids under the market. This theory may be confirmed by the higher, flat consistency of the 50-day moving average.

> **Cooper** is a trading pattern based on the often-occurring 1-2-3 pattern with an extra kicker day, resulting in the pattern 1-2-3 + 1.

By April 2, you see the results of a three-bar surge on a pullback. In the 1-2-3 pullback by the end of the chart—the handle—you also see a fourth day in the trend, followed by an NR7. These combine to confirm what is about to happen: a strong upward surge. I call the 1-2-3 followed with an extra stutter step day, a cooper pattern.

The NR 7 displays the narrowest trading range out of the previous seven days. This is a classic situation. What you want to look for is multiple patterns and set-ups. These confirming patterns make it much easier to anticipate the next move.

Self-test questions

1. The three-bar surge is a signal that:

   a. It is time to get on board because a strong rally is beginning.

   b. The current trend may be coming to an end.

   c. Price support is exaggerated and is about to collapse to the downside.

   d. The trading range is expanding in a triangle formation.

2. An iguana pattern is:

   a. Simply another name for the lizard, with no other distinction.

   b. So called because it is slow-moving.

   c. Nothing more than a lizard seen on the larger weekly chart.

   d. One with a long tail, and a sign of bearish changes ahead.

3. A breakaway gap:

   a. Forms when one period's close and the next period's open are spaced apart.

   b. Typically occurs along with high volume.

   c. Is a symptom of a strong trend in the indicated direction.

   d. All of the above.

4. A day trader is one who:

   a. Buys stock and holds for at least one day, often selling in the following trading period.
   b. Buys and sells within a single trading day, usually closing positions by the close of the session.
   c. Believes that specific days are stronger market days than others, and will buy only on those days of the week.
   d. Only buys stocks reporting profits (day) and never those reporting losses (night).

5. A narrow range trading period is one that:

   a. Shows little space between opening and closing prices and little or no trading activity above or below those levels.
   b. Is dominated by buy or sell activity only in a stock with a chronically small trading range.
   c. Has primary trading activity among institutions, so that few trades occur but volume is quite high.
   d. Is typical of investor uncertainty or confusion, usually preceding a strong bear market.

For answers, go to www.traderslibrary.com/TLEcorner

Chapter 4
Anticipating the Next Move

While the market demonstrates patterns of threes and sevens, it sometimes pauses in between. This makes identification of the pattern elusive at times and much more interesting. The pause can be a deceptive reality in price patterns. To anticipate the next move, you need to recognize not only the precise patterns, but also the tempo and delay that often accompany them.

Recognizing Patterns, Tempo, and Delay

For example, if we take a look at the daily chart for Expedia, you will see what I mean (figure 4.1).

FIGURE 4.1 - EXPE–EXPEDIA Inc.–Daily.

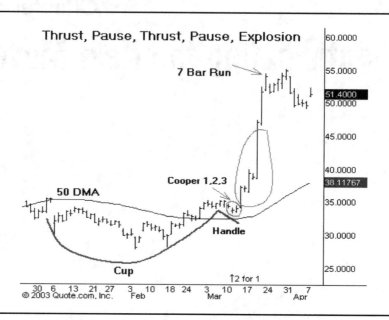

December 26, 2002 thru April 7, 2003
For larger view, go to www.traderslibrary.com/TLEcorner

This pattern involves two thrusts and a pivot, and quite a pivot at that. I call this pattern an explosion. But note that the three steps are interspaced with pauses as well. It would be a nice world if all patterns could be easily identified and timed, but that is not the world we live in. This pattern plays out below the 50-day moving average, and then takes off, soaring far above it. This formation tells you several things. For the immediate future—the price pattern beyond this specific chart—you probably have to realize that price is going to retreat back to the 50 DMA level.

It starts out with a very clear cup and handle formation. Note the test of the cup-shaped bottom, with support moving in the cup pattern; the move above the 50 DMA which forms a small handle; and then the big explosion over a 7-day period—the classic 7-bar run.

The Running Cup and Handle

Returning for the moment to the earlier section of the chart, note the symmetry at the cup and handle phase. We see numerous three-stage moves here. The 7-bar run is preceded by a Cooper 1-2-3. I call this specific formation a running cup and handle. This is simply because of its proximity to the 50 DMA. With consolidation beneath the moving average, the price then moves above to form what I call a high handle because it takes place above the average whereas the cup was below.

> **Running cup and handle** is a formation in which the cup forms in consolidation entirely beneath but very close to the 50-day moving average, and the handle forms completely above the same average.

The 7-bar run is in a strong uptrend, which is why I call it a price explosion. In another formation you can use to anticipate price movement, you see a plus-one, minus-two version of the three-part move. The next chart gives you an example of this (figure 4.2).

The Lexmark daily chart concludes with a plus-one, minus-two pattern. It sets up an entry to the stock. Many day traders entered into the market in the period from 1998 to 2000 and used numer-

FIGURE 4.2 - LXK–Lexmark Int'l. Inc.–Daily

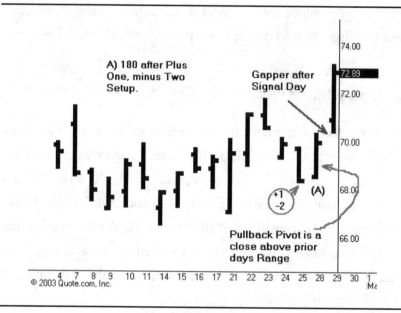

A) 180 after Plus
One, minus Two
Setup.

Gapper after
Signal Day

74.00

72.89

72.00

70.00

+1
-2

(A)

68.00

Pullback Pivot is a
close above prior
days Range

66.00

© 2003 Quote.com, Inc.

4 7 8 9 10 11 14 15 16 17 21 22 23 24 25 28 29 30 1
Ma

April 4, 2003 thru April 29, 2003
For larger view, go to www.traderslibrary.com/TLEcorner

ous charting formations to find set-up signals. Most believed you
should wait for a tick above the prior day's high to confirm the set-
up. But there are many ways to skin a cat.

> **High handle** is a handle segment of the cup and handle in which the
> handle forms entirely above the moving average.

Opening Range Breakouts

With the plus-one, minus-two formation, you can look for an opportunity to go long in a few ways. I like to look for an opening

range breakout here, which is a breakout above the first three 10-minute bars.

> **Opening range breakout** is a breakout formation occurring on a day above an uptrend or below a downtrend, after the first three 10-minute bars.

Pullback Pivots

The breakout can also occur on the daily chart, of course, and that is strong confirmation as well. The gapper taking place after the signal day confirms the buy set-up. But look for a moment to the previous day on this chart; you see a pullback pivot closing above the prior day's range. So there is a signal and two different confirming patterns. The signal is the plus-one, minus-two, and the two confirmations are the pullback pivot and the breakout. When it comes to signals and confirmations, if you wait too long, you could miss your chance.

> **Pullback pivot** is a bar showing a reversal in the trend and a pivot, with a close on the opposite side of the range from the previous day; a confirmation of the price direction.

Even if you don't make a move from this initial set-up at the plus-one, minus-two, you certainly recognize the pullback pivot.

The gap-and-go after the signal day confirms the confirmation in a sense. It proves that the pullback pivot was a legitimate signal, but by the time you see this, it's too late to make your move. This is also what I call a 180 set-up, noted at point A in figure 4.2. There's a close in the top area of the day's range after the previous day's close right at the bottom of the range—a 180.

Opening Range Bar Reversals

We can also see an opening range bar reversal which goes beyond the usual three-bar formation. This is a signal that the three-bar trend is pausing, but is likely to continue as well. Here's an example for Lexmark shown on the 10-minute chart (figure 4.3).

The opening range bar (ORB) breaks downward through support on this chart; and then the price moves upward strongly, ultimately breaking through resistance on the other side. So the day starts out with a bar going down through support, and a reversal moving up through resistance. In the chartist community, this is a classic example of a downside attempt failing and leading to a strong— very strong—uptrend.

> **Opening range bar reversal** is a bar moving opposite the three-bar trend indicating a pause in that trend and likely continuation afterwards.

This kind of formation tells me to be on my toes during the trading day. Big things are going to happen. Opportunities and risks are there, and I have to pay close attention to the signals to know when or if to make my move. The reversal might simply be a knee-jerk reaction to the opening price decline; so, looking at the chart only

FIGURE 4.3 - LXK–Lexmark Int'l. Inc.–10-minute

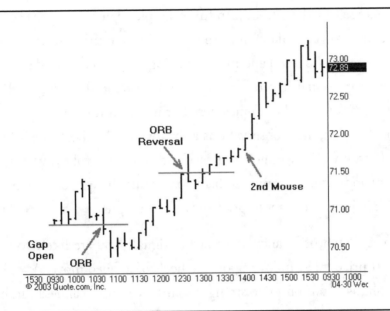

April 29, 2003
For larger view, go to www.traderslibrary.com/TLEcorner

to the point of the reversal may not show the full picture of what's going on. The volatility might trouble you. But then you see the second mouse—remember the second mouse is the one that gets the cheese—it confirms that the reversal is for real.

The Hour of Truth

This is a good example of a phenomenon I have observed over and over in pattern analysis. After an opening range bar reversal, the validity of what this implies will be set within one hour. If the trend sticks for the hour, then the stock will usually close that day at or near the top of the range (if an uptrend) or at or near the bottom of the range (if a downtrend). In this example (figure 4.3), you see an opening range breakdown to the downside, a turndown, and then a reversal in the trend and in the opening range. The second mouse is your go signal if you haven't moved yet. And don't forget, I'm giving you uptrend examples here but if you turn the whole thing upside down, these observations also work on the short side. I like to keep my signals quick and easy and not get involved with too many indicators. I always go back to my rule that price is the final arbiter. I need to react to price through the signals.

If you watch price and interpret the signals, you are likely to see a fast price move following on the heels of a failed move. A lot of emphasis is put on price strength, but preceding weakness can be just as important. This was the case for Quicksilver, as shown in its daily chart (figure 4.4).

Quicksilver was poised to roll over and break down. In fact, by mid-day, the pattern was starting to look like a classic head and shoulders formation. As it began moving down off the high, it looked like a strong downtrend. But then, at the end of the chart we saw, instead, the same 180 and then (at A) a gap at the next session.

Gap-and-Go

The rollover set-up is followed by a pullback pivot. When the price did gap-and-go the next day, it meant that there was either strong

FIGURE 4.4 - ZQK–Quicksilver Cp–Daily

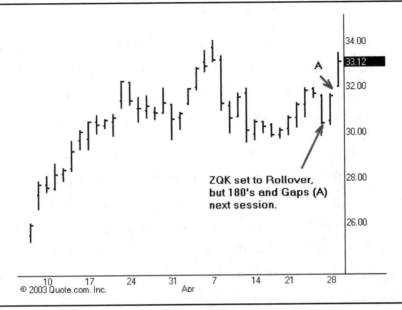

ZQK set to Rollover, but 180's and Gaps (A) next session.

© 2003 Quote.com. Inc.

April 6, 2003 thru April 29, 2003
For larger view, go to www.traderslibrary.com/TLEcorner

buying pressure or a lot of short positions being squeezed. We really can't tell which one of these is at work behind this because the pattern looks the same in both instances. And actually, we don't care either, as long as we get in at the right time and when price is moving in the right direction.

> **Head and shoulders** is a chart pattern involving three tests of resistance (with the middle higher than the first and third) followed by a retreat; or, in a reverse of the pattern, three tests of support followed by an advance.

Anticipating the Next Move | 49

Let's take a look at the 10-minute chart of the gap-and-go on this stock (figure 4.5). Some interesting 1-2-3 development took place on this day and it is worth more study.

The day started out with a very, very strong gap-and-go, not only from the previous day but on a second gap right after the open. The high point (1) culminates a three-bar surge. But with this kind of price formation, how do you know when to get out? What is the sell set-up?

I use a number of signals for sell set-ups. I like to observe measured moves, such as a two-point move in the morning followed by a pullback. When I see this, I conclude that the stock is probably going to have a trend day. By this I mean the direction has been set early on and I expect that to continue through to closing, even with offsetting pullbacks.

I also look for symmetrical two-point moves later in the day or three-point drives to a high point (on the long side) or low point (on the short). Day traders and swing traders also like this kind of formation. So for example, at point 1, you have a classic sell signal because it follows a four-day uptrend (higher highs offset by higher lows). Then you see a narrow day followed by a reversal day. The high point is followed by a classic three-day downtrend, so day and swing traders will tell you that the following narrow range day is a clear buy signal. And sure enough, the stock continues upward to point 2. Then you see the extremely narrow day, a sell signal once again. After this decline, it is a little more difficult to find the buy

FIGURE 4.5 · ZQK–Quicksilver Cp–10-minute

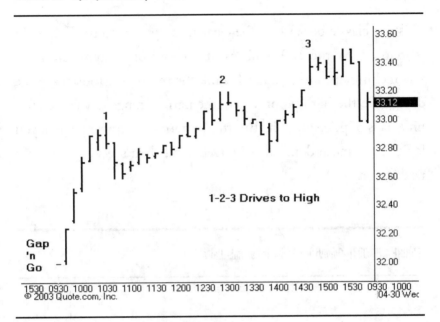

April 29, 2003
For larger view, go to www.traderslibrary.com/TLEcorner

set-up, but that relatively large down day at the bottom followed by the up day works. Sure enough, price rose again to point 3 and was immediately followed by another narrow range day. So I agree with day traders and swing traders that the 1-2-3 patterns are very dependable.

The 1-2-3 and Pullback Pattern

Let's look at another example of how a trend goes through the 1-2-3 and then goes into a pullback position. OmniVision Technologies showed this classic pattern on the next daily chart example (figure 4.6).

This is a classic because of the clear three-part pattern. The 1-2-3 is followed by the 180 pullback at the end of a day where price was inching upward steadily. I think the sell set-up took place the day before the high point, where the narrow range day came after nine days of price growth. But this pattern is interesting when you look at the more detailed daily chart and then see what happens next (figure 4.7).

FIGURE 4.6 - OVTI–OmniVision Technologies Inc.–Daily

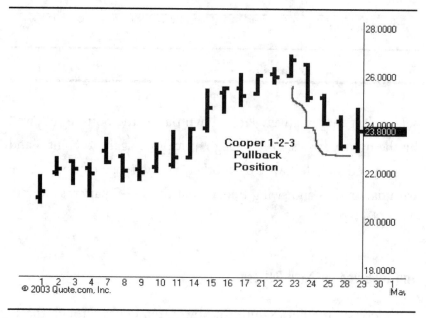

April 1, 2003 thru April 29, 2003
For larger view, go to www.traderslibrary.com/TLEcorner

The Catapult

The next day, when the stock should be ready to go up, it moves downward, marginally taking out the prior day's low. When it goes red like this against what most people's expectations were, I call it a catapult because as soon as the trend turns, it is going to go strongly in the opposite direction.

In figure 4.7, the following day shows a steadily declining 1-2-3 pattern, a drive to the low. Then the price rises to the opening range bar (ORB) point and climbs strongly to a new high before

FIGURE 4.7 · OVTI–OmniVision Technologies Inc.–10-minute

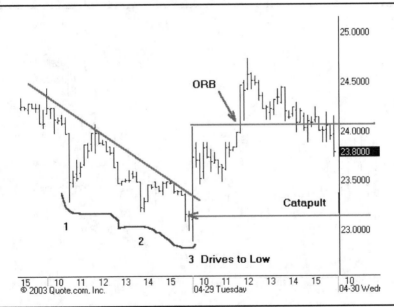

Late afternoon on April 27, 2003 thru April 29, 2003

retreating. In this formation, as soon as the price turns at the low, I recommend buying with a trailing stop and riding it upward.

> **Catapult** is a formation of price movement in an unexpected direction, followed by an exceptionally strong and fast price reversal.

Using Pattern Identification Tools to Time Set-Ups

You can use these pattern identification tools to time your set-up expertly. Let me show you another example, going back to the

FIGURE 4.8 - PGTV–Pegasus Communications Corporation–Daily

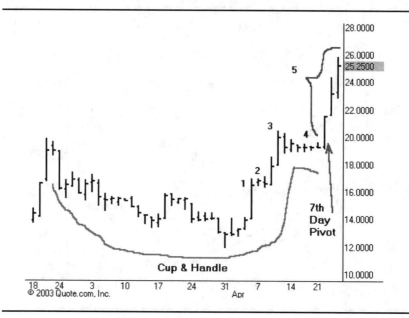

February 18, 2003 thru April 24, 2003
For larger view, go to www.traderslibrary.com/TLEcorner

cup and handle (figure 4.8). Pegasus Communications went through many days of consolidation in its 'cup' period in three drives to the low.

After this, the 1-2-3 reversal went to a high and then formed a 7-day handle with virtually no price change. Note the progressive narrow range days while investors tried to figure out what to do next. This is the classic "thrust, pause, thrust" formation. The 7th day sees the pivot and a very strong continuation to the upside. Price literally exploded from point 4 to 5 and continued upward.

FIGURE 4.9 - PGTV–Pegasus Communications Corporation–Hourly

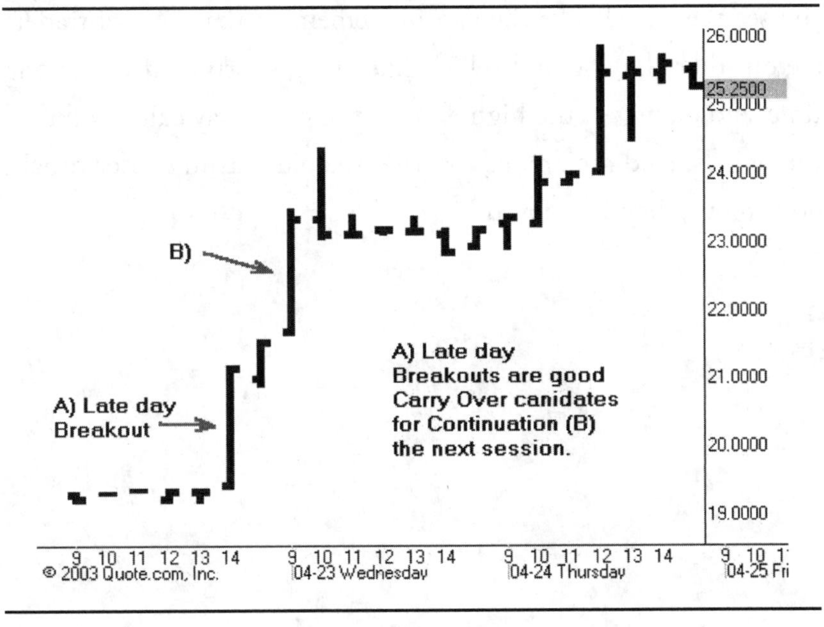

A) Late day Breakouts are good Carry Over canidates for Continuation (B) the next session.

A) Late day Breakout

B)

© 2003 Quote.com, Inc.

April 22, 2003 thru April 24, 2003

You can get better insight into this explosion by looking at the hourly chart for these days (figure 4.9).

The late-day breakout takes the stock upward, and here it is important to observe that late-day breakouts are likely to see continuation of the trend the following day. That's exactly what happened here. So if you took your buy set-up at the indicated place the day before, you can ride this up to the top. The sell set-up takes place right at that high day when you have already seen three uptrend days followed by the lower close.

This is followed by nearly two days of uncertainty. But then there are three uptrend hours at midday Thursday, another buy set-up taking the price to a new high by the end of the session. So when you see the signals like the gap-up, remember that a lot of traders are out there buying and selling like crazy, shorting at the wrong time, and buying at the high. Follow the price, stay calm, and read the signals. And remember, too, that the old maxim works: Stocks don't move, they are moved.

Self-test questions

1. The running cup and handle is a formation in which:

   a. The formation looks the same as the normal cup and handle, but turned upside down and foreshadowing a price decline.

   b. The handle precedes the cup instead of following it.

   c. The cup pattern is angled and trending upward or downward rather than the more traditional level pattern.

   d. The cup forms in consolidation under the moving average, and the handle forms above the moving average.

2. An opening range breakout is:

   a. A breakout formation occurring above the uptrend or below the downtrend established by the first three 10-minute bars.

   b. An opening gap from the prior day, in which an established trend is contradicted.

   c. Not likely to be sustainable throughout the day, because the moving average forces the price to return to established trading range levels.

   d. A signal that the day's trading will be highly volatile, especially if accompanied by exceptionally high volume.

3. A pullback pivot is:

   a. A momentary pause in the current trend, followed by a strong return to the established direction.
   b. Meaningless if not confirmed by narrow range day or convergence of moving averages.
   c. A reversal in the current trend, with trading closing on the side of the range opposite from the previous day.
   d. That portion of the cup and handle where the handle bends downward rather than moving horizontally.

4. The head and shoulders pattern consists of:

   a. Tests of resistance in three stages, followed by an upside breakout.
   b. Moving in price that test of resistance or support during highly volatile price movement, usually indicating a struggle between buyers and sellers and foreshadowing a period of price uncertainty.
   c. Three tests of resistance followed by downward price movement; or three tests of support followed by upward price movement.
   d. Buyer strength in a middle price spike offset by seller strength at preceding and following ledges, or shoulders, indicating general agreement about the breadth of the current trading range.

5. A trend day is one in which:

   a. An early-day measured price move is likely to continue on the same trend throughout the entire day.

   b. Both upward and downward price trends are witnessed and offsetting one another.

   c. The previous day's trend is always continued as part of a longer-term trend.

   d. Many breakouts are seen as a strong indication of a new trend being formed, identifying that day as the starting point of a long-term reversal.

For answers, go to www.traderslibrary.com/TLEcorner

Chapter 5

Triangulating the Trend

Chart pattern recognition is not an easy task. You cannot always respond to the same moves in the same way. It is a cryptic matter. Why? Because even when you see strong gap-ups, it's not caused by genuine buying. Market makers are able, by virtue of their position, to manipulate short-term prices.

This distorts what you see and may deceive you. This is why it is essential to master some additional pattern trends. Let's start with the Adtran daily chart (figure 5.1).

Triangles

Fast moves develop from failed moves. Remember that. One pattern that reveals a lot is the often-seen triangle. Recognition is only the first step. You should next be asking: What happens when the stock breaks down after a triangle forms in one direction, and then quickly moves in the opposite direction? And by "quickly," I'm talking about one to three days in terms of daily chart analysis. That's one to three bars. Look for situations where the stock moves strongly right after the triangle and takes out the upper triangle levels to the upside or the bottom levels on the downside.

The triangle may ascend or descend and be followed by a breakout above or below. These factors make triangles difficult to read, but

FIGURE 5.1 - ADTN—ADTRAN Inc.—Daily

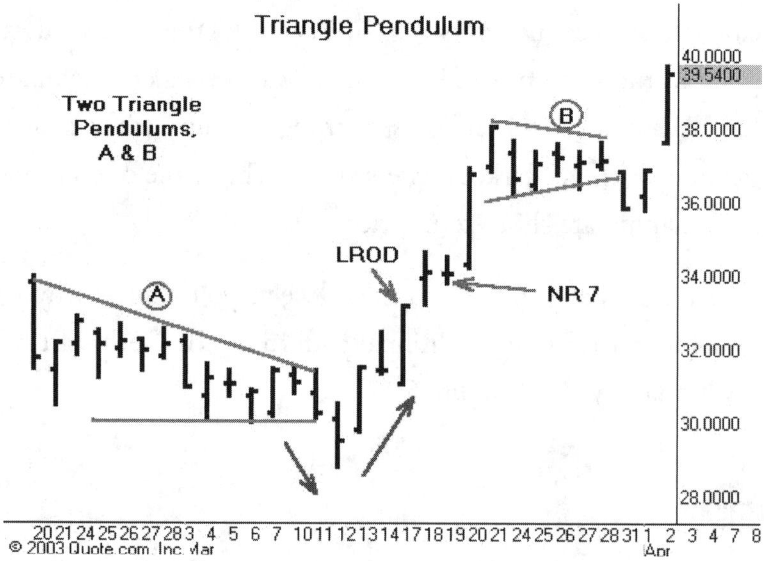

Triangle Pendulum

February 20, 2003 thru April 2, 2003
For larger view, go to www.traderslibrary.com/TLEcorner

if you know a few points about the triangle and how to interpret them, the job becomes easier.

> **Failed moves patterns** are exhibited when price attempts to move in a particular direction, but is not able to sustain it. Such moves often precede moves in the opposite direction.

Adtran's daily chart is a classic failed move pattern. Note the first triangle forming at A. The price declines and narrows in a classic descending triangle pattern, and then breaks to the upside. This kind of pattern emerges at times when institutions want to buy shares but they are scarce. So market makers work with the institutions to help break down the stock looking for weak holders, anyone willing to sell once prices are depressed. The idea is that once that price declines, the institutions move in and buy cheap shares. But because this results from short-term manipulation, it often doesn't hold up—just as it happened here.

> **Triangle** is a pattern of trading in which the trading range narrows over a number of periods, usually resulting in a decisive move beyond the triangle's upper or lower borders.

Large Range Outside Day

In this case, the triangle is followed by the development of a large range outside day (LROD). This is what candlestick chartists call an engulfing line because the range is higher and lower than the previous day's trading range.

In this case, the LROD day is also a 180. The previous day closed near the low, but this day closed at the high. So you see here a multiple set-up, even though it doesn't develop on the following day. But on the second day, you find another familiar pattern, an NR7. If you check the last day of the triangle and then count forward to the narrow range day, you see the classic seven-bar pattern, and this confirms what happens next. The seven-day pattern moves into a three-day pattern. The NR7 is the first day followed by two additional uptrend days, ending in the formation of yet another triangle, noted at B.

The volatility set-up starting at the NR7 defines the pattern to follow, but it also confirms what is implied before. So the moral of this story is clear: You cannot just watch one bar. You have to understand emerging patterns as they appear over a period of time. You need to put the pieces together, creating the puzzle so you can see the whole picture. In this case, the chart ends with a breakout duplicating the pattern after the first triangle. Apply what you figured out from one triangle to the second one occurring less than two weeks later.

Large range outside day (LROD) is a trading day in which the trading range is both higher and lower than the preceding day's range, also called an engulfing line in candlestick terminology.

The Triangle Pendulum

The NR7 is, indeed, a powerful set-up for what I call the triangle pendulum. Both of the triangles on this chart meet that definition. It occurs when the triangle ends with the bottom taken out, as occurred in both of these, and then a strong reversal upward The same can occur in the opposite direction, with the pendulum swinging upward to take out the top and then falling back below.

> **Pendulum** is a pattern in which the triangle ends with movement below the trading range, followed by a price surge or above the trading range, followed by a price decline.

So in figure 5.1 you had two triangles, both breaking below the range and then, in the pendulum move, reversing and moving upward. You see even more volatility in the same stock in the period following, as shown on the next chart (figure 5.2).

Here Adtran moves from its late June low to demonstrate that the triangle pendulum was a false undercut. To expand our vocabulary even farther, I call this pattern the boomerang. You often see this effect, an extreme move and reversal, right before a major move. It's also called a WV bottom because of its shape, and it precedes a strong price uptrend. On the top side you see the opposite, an MA top, which precedes a price decline.

The triangle pendulum often acts in the role of a false undercut, as we see at the beginning of this chart. So what looks like a triangle

FIGURE 5.2 · ADTN–ADTRAN Inc.–Daily Chart #2

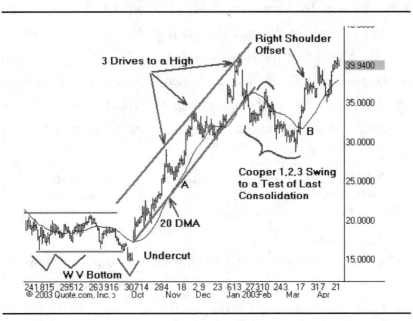

June 20, 2003 thru April 23, 2003
For larger view, go to www.traderslibrary.com/TLEcorner

formation is actually a flat. The bottom is taken out, in this case by the V segment of the WV. But then, when the boomerang swings around and takes out the top of the flat, you see real momentum.

Let's analyze this pattern further. Note how the 20-day moving average cushions the strength and rides all the way up in three drives to the high. A 1-2-3 pattern, again. This is a mirror image of the WV. A three-part bottom is followed by a three-part drive in the opposite direction, which is something you see again and again. Then after the high is reached, you see another 1-2-3 swing to a test of your previous consolidation—another classic pattern. It's as though the market isn't sure about the uptrend, so it takes a test or a breather before resuming. Swing traders and day traders like these kinds of patterns because the set-ups are easy to spot.

Also note the 1-2-3 test forms an inverted head and shoulders. There are three descending tests at the bottom ending at B and then a strong offset to the right shoulder. Remember, the head and shoulders pattern tests in one direction right before price moves in the opposite direction. Here a bottom formation tests support and then takes off. It is also fascinating and—from a trader's point of

> **Inverted head and shoulders** is a head and shoulders pattern with tests of support rather than of resistance.

view, comforting—to watch how the 20 DMA acts. It tracks the moves quite nicely and, right at the bottom of the test (again, at B) the 20 DMA reasserts itself and again tracks the price upward.

FIGURE 5.3 - ADTN–ADTRAN Inc.–Hourly Chart 1

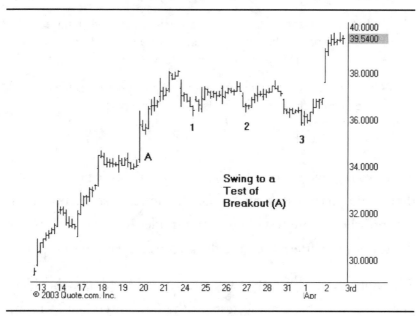

March 13, 2003 thru April 2, 2003
For larger view, go to www.traderslibrary.com/TLEcorner

Recognizing Repetitive Patterns

Let's look at the last segment of this pattern on an hourly chart (figure 5.3). This is very revealing and shows how a swing leads to a test of breakout.

This chart demonstrates the point that specific patterns tend to repeat themselves on all time scales. Here we see a consolidation at the beginning, two distinct thrusts, a slight pause going into point A, and then a 1-2-3 swing. The 1-2-3 is a buy set-up followed by a breakout and a strong surge to the upside.

FIGURE 5.4 -ADTN–ADTRAN Inc.–Hourly Chart 2

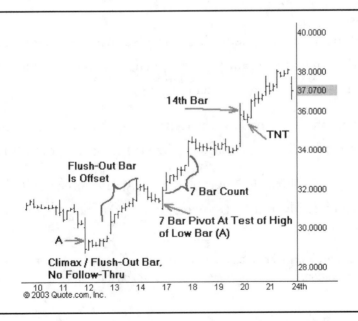

March 10, 2003 thru March 21, 2003

We see another example of repetitive patterns on a second hourly chart for Adtran, shown in the next figure (figure 5.4).

Note that hourly chart patterns look the same as the daily charts, but on an accelerated time scale. There was a lot going on here, as my analysis shows. This chart provides some great examples of how sevens play out on charts, and how they interact with patterns of threes.

The chart begins with a flat period and then a drop at 'A', which I call a flush-out bar. But you see that there is no downside fol-

---

Flush-out bar is a bar moving strongly above or below a range, usually singular and followed by a trend in the opposite direction.

---

low-through. In fact, the flush-out is offset with a strong uptrend, which often occurs. Remember the phenomenon of the pendulum and the reaction of the boomerang.

After the offset, you find a pivot at the seventh bar, and then a seven-bar uptrend—again—pausing and then rising again to the 14th bar.

And typically, this is followed by the thrust and turndown (TNT). Then, predictably in such a strong uptrend, you find a continuation.

Runaway pattern is a strong trend pattern in which the stock's direction continues strongly even with consolidation, pivots, and flush-out bars.

These are typical signs when the stock is in a runaway pattern. It gives you the sweet spot over and over at the pivots and at the offsets. And that is where you can make the fastest profits. And that's what we want, isn't it?

Self-test questions

1. A failed move occurs when:

   a. Institutional buyers do not provide interest in support of retail investor buy or sell decisions.

   b. Price movement occurs in one direction but cannot be sustained.

   c. Corporate stock issues cannot hold their IPO value.

   d. A well-recognized pattern implies movement in one direction but stock prices move the other way.

2. A triangle pattern is:

   a. A narrowing of the trading range at top and bottom, often preceding a strong price movement above or below the triangle's range.

   b. A sign of growing investor interest in the stock, with volatility levels increasing over time until a price gap precedes breakout.

   c. Descriptive of highly volatile patterns moving upward and downward in what can be described as triangular in nature.

   d. The name given by chartists to the decline in stock price when earnings fall short of expectations.

3. A long range outside day (LROD) is:

   a. Another name for what candlestick chartists call the engulfing line.
   b. A day when the trading range moves higher than the highest point of the prior day.
   c. A day when the trading range moves lower than the lowest point of the prior day.
   d. All of the above.

4. A pendulum and a boomerang are similar in the sense that:

   a. Both involve high volatility in all instances.
   b. They display the forces of panic when stock prices plummet.
   c. Both involve initial movement in one direction, followed by an offset in the opposite direction.
   d. All of the above.

5. A WV bottom is a:

   a. Term describing descending prices with Wave Volume trends.
   b. Pattern of Wide Volatility at the bottom of the trading range.
   c. Three-part test of support followed by an uptrend.
   d. Window of Value moment, preceding further decline in price.

For answers, go to www.traderslibrary.com/TLEcorner

Chapter 6

When Stocks Don't Behave As They Should

It is reassuring when the patterns set up an outcome we expect especially when we have taken a position in the stock based on those patterns. But there are times when stocks do not seem to be behaving as they should.

Case Studies
Digital River

Take a look at the daily chart for Digital River and I'll show you what I mean (figure 6.1).

Here, I like to explain this as a case of a stock putting its money where its mouth is. The downside head and shoulders also forms a

FIGURE 6.1 - DRIV–Digital River Inc.–Daily

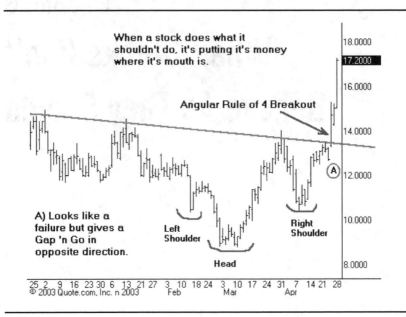

When a stock does what it
shouldn't do, it's putting it's money
where it's mouth is.

Angular Rule of 4 Breakout

A) Looks like a
failure but gives a
Gap 'n Go in
opposite direction.

Left
Shoulder

Right
Shoulder

Head

18.0000
17.2000
16.0000
14.0000
12.0000
10.0000
8.0000

25 2 9 16 23 30 6 13 21 27 3 10 18 24 3 10 17 24 31 7 14 21 28
© 2003 Quote.com, Inc. n 2003   Feb   Mar   Apr

November 11, 2002 thru April 28, 2003
For larger view, go to www.traderslibrary.com/TLEcorner

large cup and handle, so large I call it a stein and handle. It's simply
far too deep to be called a typical cup formation.

> **Stein and handle** is an unusually deep, exaggerated cup and han-
> dle formation.

A lot of day traders and swing traders can lose money when a stock
forms up like this. Why? Because there is a lot of volatility and
apparent trends going on here, but they have not lasted. You have
the numerous triple tops forming over this period, and the actual

breakout point is called the rule of 4 breakout. This was the fourth attempt to breakout above the declining resistance line. Note how that resistance has angled downward; this is an angular version of the rule of 4 breakout.

> **Rule of 4 breakout** is a breakout occurring on the fourth test of resistance (at the top) or support (at the bottom), useful as a confirming signal for other patterns, such as a preceding head and shoulders.

The rule of 4 breakout often is the first step in a very rapid move. The typical chart analyst might not have picked up on this by focusing too closely on smaller time frames, which day and swing traders tend to do. With that in mind, it also makes sense to step back and look at how a trend is developing over a larger time frame.

In this example, several signals came together at the right time. The rule of 4 breakout, the inverted head and shoulders, and the small gap at A. You could look at figure 6.1 as a series of false moves, but you should also remember that false moves lead to fast moves. In fact, a look at the hourly chart from the gap-'n-go point and forward for three days is interesting as well for what it reveals (figure 6.2).

The initial step was a very strong thrust, followed by a pause lasting nearly two days. But note how it ended: with a 14th bar pivot. Then the stock just continues upward.

FIGURE 6.2 -DRIV—Digital River Inc.—Hourly

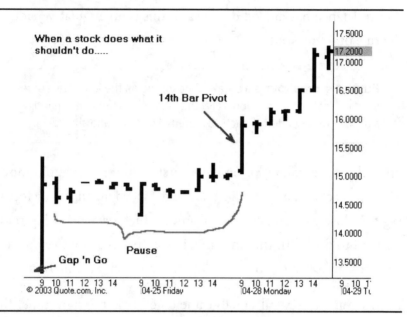

When a stock does what it
shouldn't do.....

14th Bar Pivot

Pause

Gap 'n Go

© 2003 Quote.com, Inc.   04-25 Friday   04-28 Monday   04-29 Tu

April 24, 25, 28, 2003
For larger view, go to www.traderslibrary.com/TLEcorner

MicroStrategy

Let's look at another example. The daily chart for MicroStrategy
provides you with another pattern of a stock not doing what it
should (figure 6.3). I would have expected the stock to continue
downward at A after the 1-2-3 and 180. That's the sell signal. Instead, the price took off at point B in spite of what the pattern
implied would happen. So as I cautioned you before, nothing gives
you a 100% guarantee.

FIGURE 6.3 - MSTR–MicroStrategy Inc.–Daily

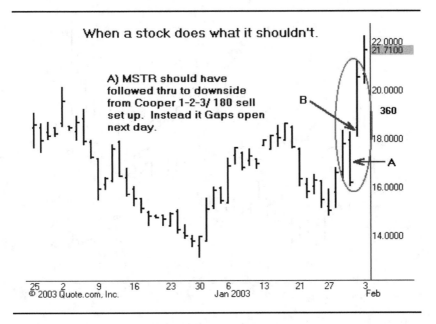

When a stock does what it shouldn't.

A) MSTR should have
followed thru to downside
from Cooper 1-2-3/ 180 sell
set up. Instead it Gaps open
next day.

B

360

A

22.0000
21.7100
20.0000
18.0000
16.0000
14.0000

25   2   9   16   23   30   6   13   21   27   3
© 2003 Quote.com, Inc.   Jan 2003   Feb

November 25, 2002 thru February 3, 2003

Borg Warner

Here's another example, seen on the daily chart of Borg Warner
(figure 6.4). First note the 50-day moving average, a steady line
with the running cup and handle forming classically: cup below,
handle above.

The handle forms up with what I call a flying wedge. That's a wedge
that looks like it's the preamble to the stock taking off. The borders are clearly downward and the pattern lasts seven bars. That's

FIGURE 6.4 - BWA–Borg Warner Inc.–Daily

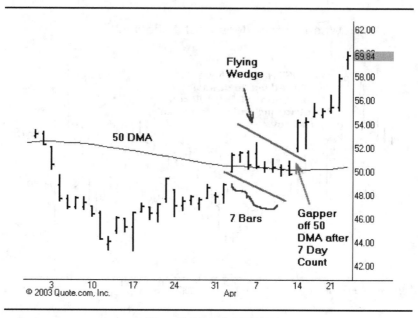

February 27, 2003 thru April 23, 2003
For larger view, go to www.traderslibrary.com/TLEcorner

a strong signal and, sure enough, the stock gaps up above the 50 DMA and takes off.

When you see the cup and handle and the handle wedges down like this, it is a sign that a strong upward move is on the horizon. We can also see just how strong the gap was in this case by looking at a micro version of the move on the 10-minute chart (figure 6.5).

Flying wedge is a wedge pattern providing a strong indication of a price move to follow, based on the pattern and bar count.

FIGURE 6.5 - BWA—Borg Warner Inc.—10-minute

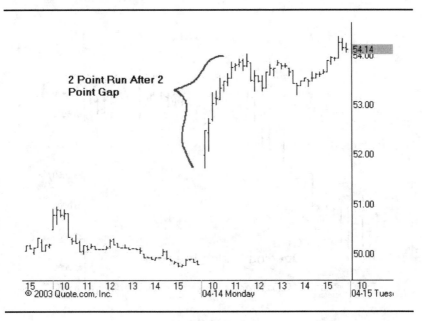

2 Point Run After 2
Point Gap

April 11 and April 14, 2003

This rather large gap raises another important question. Let's say you were fortunate to buy in before the gap. So when do you get out? Look for symmetry, that's where you find the answer. The gap was two points, followed by a two-point run. That kind of symmetry—where the point move mimics the gap distance—is a good signal that it's time to take your profits and get out.

> *"That kind of symmetry—where the point move mimics the gap distance—is a good signal that it's time to take your profits and get out."*

When Stocks Don't Behave As They Should | 81

FIGURE 6.6 - YHOO–Yahoo! Inc.–10-minute

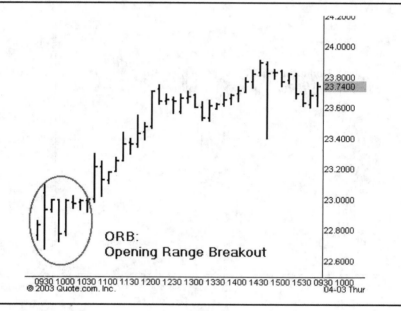

April 2, 2003
For larger view, go to www.traderslibrary.com/TLEcorner

Yahoo

You can also identify points to close by the duration of a pattern. Look at the 10-minute chart for Yahoo! to see an example of this (figure 6.6).

This was a classic opening range breakout pattern. The stock was trending and the day started out with the ORB. If the ORB sticks after the first 30 to 60 minutes of the trading day, it is quite likely to close at or near the high of the day. That is reassuring, and this

FIGURE 6.7 - URBN–Urban Outfitters Inc.–Daily

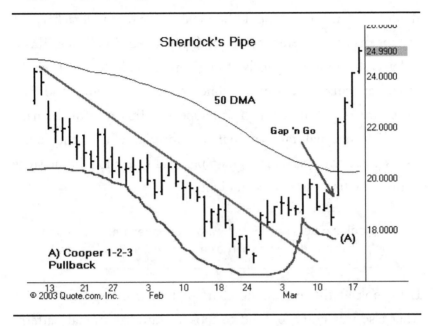

January 9, 2003 thru March 18, 2003

example proved to be true as well. So you could recognize the ORB and decide to simply ride the position through to the close. It's a dependable strategy.

Urban Outfitters

Next, let's take a look at how a pullback can signal a dramatic move. The daily chart for Urban Outfitters demonstrates another interesting pattern (figure 6.7).

In this situation, you know that the price has to rebound at some point because this sustained downward trend occurs entirely under the 50 DMA. So you should be looking for that pullback signal. It happens at A where you see the Cooper 1-2-3 pullback. This is followed by an exceptionally strong gap-'n-go. When you see the stock bouncing back after a decline, you're setting up a solid risk-to-reward play. Sure enough, it happened. This type of dramatic rise, with the small rally and pullback forming a bowl, then a fast rise is a pattern I call Sherlock's pipe. And sure enough, the stock in this situation came back smoking.

> **Sherlock's pipe** is a pattern after a long downtrend including a small rally, pullback, and dramatic gap-'n-go formation.

Let's look at the 10-minute chart of that gap-'n-go day to see what else was going on and to look for any additional patterns (figure 6.8).

It is interesting to me to note the two mini-rallies here. They both extend three points from bottom to top, a sign of exceptional strength in the uptrend. A day trader would certainly want to get a piece of that. Even if you expect the stock to continue upward, it makes sense to take some profits out of these measured moves.

The question is ever present: When should you sell? After each of the three-point moves, you have had strong momentum. If you think the stock is just going upward indefinitely, you can average buy in with more shares. Averaging on the way up is smart, but averaging on the way down is something I never recommend.

FIGURE 6.8 - URBN–Urban Outfitters Inc.–10-minute

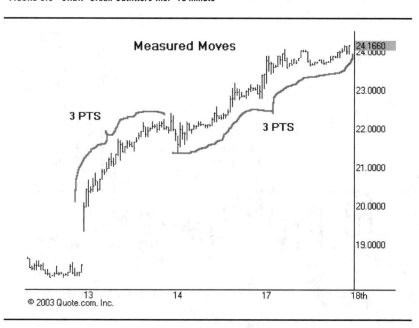

March 12, 2003 midday thru March 17, 2003
For larger view, go to www.traderslibrary.com/TLEcorner

Rent-A-Center

The gap-'n-go can follow all kinds of formations, as you have seen. Next I want to show you one occurring after a flat. I'll also explain how to recognize the signals of the breakout.

The daily chart for Rent-A-Center is interesting because of its flat leading to the breakout (figure 6.9). No one should have been surprised by this. But if you look at the first two-thirds of the chart, you can't really tell much about it because the trading range is flat

FIGURE 6.9 -RCII–Rent-A-Center Inc.–Daily

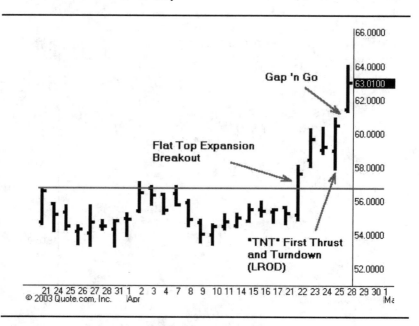

March 21, 2003 thru April 28, 2003
For larger view, go to www.traderslibrary.com/TLEcorner

for such an extended period of time. But the breakout occurs at the point where you see the largest bar in 10 days, a sign that something is changing. The fact that price breaks to the upside is encouraging, and the direction is confirmed by the thrust and turndown that follows immediately. This can be seen as confirmation of the large-bar day, and the instinct proves right when the next day turns into a gap-'n-go formation. When you look at the 10-minute chart for that Friday-Monday two-day move, you get a bird's-eye view of the signal itself (figure 6.10).

FIGURE 6.10 · RCII–Rent-A-Center Inc.–10-minute

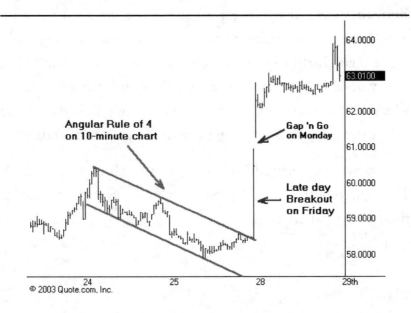

April 24, 25, & 28, 2003

Note the downward angular rule of 4 preceding the move and a late-day breakout on Friday. Those declining tops on the rule of four tell you something is coming and sure enough, the breakout took place at the fourth try. So you have a flying wedge ending with a rule of 4 turnaround, a late day breakout, and then—on the next trading day—a gap-'n-go.

Friday Afternoon Breakouts

Breakouts, particularly on Friday afternoons, are great carryover candidates because everyone starts out Monday morning looking at their charts. Money managers are going into meetings late Friday or early Monday. People are talking over the weekend. So when you see a breakout like this, hopefully not in hindsight, you can expect to see an interesting pattern emerging on Monday.

Sometimes the weekend isn't time off as much as time to think. This little tip can lead to big profits if you're paying attention to these Friday patterns.

Self-test questions

1. The rule of 4 breakout is an observation that:

    a. a breakout frequently occurs on the fourth test of resistance or support.
    b. most breakout patterns are limited to a move of four points before reversal.
    c. A breakout lasting four days or less is a false signal.
    d. The four bars preceding a breakout should be moving in a direction away from the breakout itself, to confirm that it is not a false signal.

2. A flying wedge is:

    a. An evolving bearish signal invariably leading to disintegration of support levels and a strong decline to follow.
    b. A volatile formation occurring high about the 50 DMA.
    c. A pattern often foreshadowing a strong price move in the direction opposite that of the wedge.
    d. The reverse formation of the cup and handle, with the handle occurring before the cup and wedging into the cup pattern.

3. Sherlock's Pipe is a reference to:

    a. Any pattern dominated by the appearance of substance (the smoke) growing from an apparent rally that later collapses.
    b. The formation of a bearish decline (downward stem) into a consolidation pattern (pipe) before continuing downward.
    c. The charting work developed in London in the late 1800s (the era of Sherlock Holmes) and the society of chartists involved in that study.
    d. A pattern following a sustained downtrend, with a short rally and pullback and then an exceptionally rapid and strong gap-'n-go formation.

4. When a cup and handle formation is unusually deep:

    a. It is called a stein and handle.
    b. It implies that the stock is undergoing a period of improving liquidity.
    c. The obvious ramifications are bearish.
    d. The pattern is referred to as a "Bowl of Soup."

5. The inverted head and shoulders:

    a. Is a test of resistance, leading to a decline in the price.

    b. Is a test of support, leading to a rise in the price.

    c. Typically occurs in a period of consolidation and tests neither side of the trading range.

    d. Is so-called because it is a strongly bearish signal.

For answers, go to www.traderslibrary.com/TLEcorner

Chapter 7

Powerful Patterns

Now I'm going to introduce some jarring language to the discussion. At times, a pattern requires an especially graphic term to describe what is going on.

The Grenade

For example, check the daily chart for j2 Global Communications (figure 7.1).

This is an example of a strong, consistent uptrend, and you can spot the short-term swings in price that day that swing traders love. But the overall trend is up, with price moving higher and higher for 21 days (a multiple of 7, you notice)—and then you see a huge gap below support. Because this blows up the pattern, I call it a grenade.

> **Grenade** is a sudden move below support or above resistance level with a large gap, which blows up the established trend line.

How could you have anticipated this breakaway gap and moved out of the position before it hit? Most swing traders will follow the prescribed two- to five-day in-and-out rule, looking to profit in short-term moves. So if you were a swing trader in this formation, you would have taken profits at any of the short-term price peaks where sell set-ups occurred. For example, there was a three-day up-trend from days three through five, an upward price gap between

FIGURE 7.1 - JCOM–J2 Global Communications Inc.–Daily

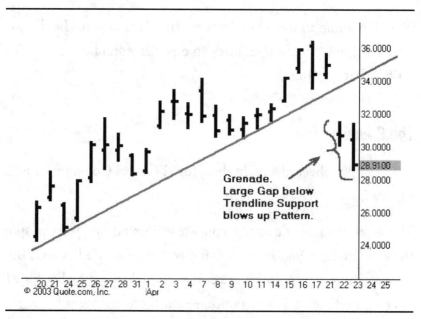

Grenade.
Large Gap below
Trendline Support
blows up Pattern.

© 2003 Quote.com, Inc.

March 20, 2003 thru April 23, 2003
For larger view, go to www.traderslibrary.com/TLEcorner

days nine and ten, and a five-day uptrend close to the end of the chart (with the grenade occurring on the seventh day after that uptrend began). So there were plenty of sell set-up signals along the way. Ideally, the swing trading approach would have been to sell at each of those points, and then re-enter the position when buy set-ups appeared.

You see this pattern's consequences emerge with clarity in the 10-minute chart for the last day of the broader chart (figure 7.2).

FIGURE 7.2 - JCOM–j2 Global Communications Inc.–10-minute

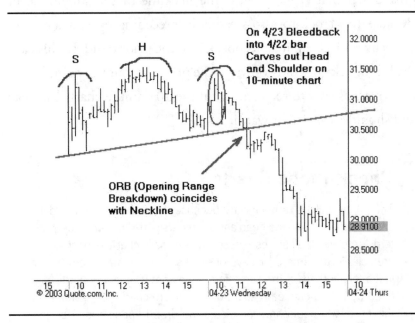

April 22, 2003 thru April 23, 2003

A Bleedback

Note how the shoulders and head of a classic head and shoulders form throughout the day of the 22nd (the first day of the grenade). If you were in this stock and decided to hold on hoping the price was going to rebound, this formation would have been a red flag to get out right away.

> **Bleedback** is a formation in which price levels return to previously established ranges after an unusual move upward or downward. The price bleeds back to the previously established trading level.

Then on the following day, April 23, you see an opening range breakdown that crosses below the neckline of the support level. Because this stock rose so steadily in preceding days, when it retreats like this, I call it a bleedback into the prior trend. In this case, the bleedback goes only down to the prior day, but the point here is that this was easy to see coming on the 10-minute chart. The head and shoulders was your warning.

Check Those Charts

Thorough analysis is necessary because if you used only the daily chart, you didn't see the head and shoulders pattern. Remember, patterns emerge on all scales. Those who like daily charts expect to see predictable patterns over days or weeks, whereas the micro trader looks for—and finds—the same formations on 10-minute charts. You need both. You can learn a lot from the micro chart. For example, in this case, you could have predicted the drop in price based on the head and shoulders formation.

Expansion Volume Breakout

Let's check another one. The CheckFree Corporation daily chart provides a typical small cup and handle with little excitement in the price pattern (figure 7.3). In fact, in this instance, I cite volume as yet another confirming indicator. I don't refer to volume that often, but I always like to check for those unusual situations where it does confirm an odd occurrence.

In this case, you see the TNT and 180 and then a gap-'n-go, which happens a lot. But at point A you also see something else: A case of

FIGURE 7.3 - CKFR–CheckFree Corporation–Daily.

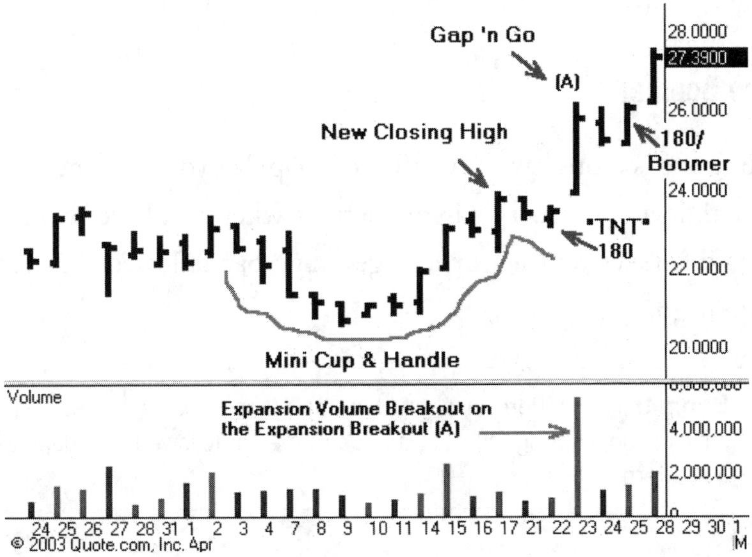

April 24, 2003 thru April 28, 2003
For larger view, go to www.traderslibrary.com/TLEcorner

expansion volume breakout, which is very important to anticipating the next move in this stock. Volume is a confirming indicator, but it also acts as a clue for what comes next.

> **Expansion volume breakout** is a price breakout accompanied with unusually high volume on the same day, usually a very strong signal. On the upside, this is strongly bullish; on the downside, it is strongly bearish.

Volume broke out at the same time as price. If you missed the prior signals, this clearly tells you that you're seeing a strong uptrend. Look at the collection of signals. There was a new closing high, following by a TNT and 180, then a gap-'n-go on high volume. You can't ask for more signals than that.

The Boomer

But there is more. Two days after the gap day, you see another 180, this time a boomer. This is the pattern when you have two inside bars inside a breakout, or a large range bar followed by another gap-'n-go.

> **Boomer** is a pattern involving two inside bars inside a breakout, anticipating a strong move; or a large range bar followed by a gap-'n-go pattern.

The signals in this case were quite clear and they came in multiples. It should have been plenty of confirmation for anyone. But things are not always so clear. It can also occur that when a stock begins breaking down, it returns to the "scene of the crime." Putting this another way, if a trend moves too far too quickly, it has to adjust. Now, I like to use uptrends to make these points, but remember the same argument works on the downside as well.

I like to remind people—again—that their first loss is their best loss. By this I mean don't hold onto a stock that moves downward unexpected, hoping it will rebound. Cut your losses as soon as possible and accept the fact that you won't always have perfect timing. If you are patient, you'll have another shot at that stock and you will improve your timing with experience. (And remember, "experience" is what you get when you were expecting something else.)

The Power Surge Formation

Let me show you an example of what can happen when a stock goes through a power surge formation—a strong thrust in one direction with little or no pause.

The daily chart for Hi-Tech Pharmacal starts out with its March high and declines to point 0 (figure 7.4). Note how narrow the trading ranges are over the following two weeks and how little the stock moves. It does provide some hints, however, inching upward. But you see this subtle 1-2-3 hint attempting to test support, preceding the power surge. Its first strong signal is the TNT right after 3, which is followed by a small gap, a breakout over double

FIGURE 7.4 - CHITK–HI-Tech Pharmacal Co. Inc.–Daily

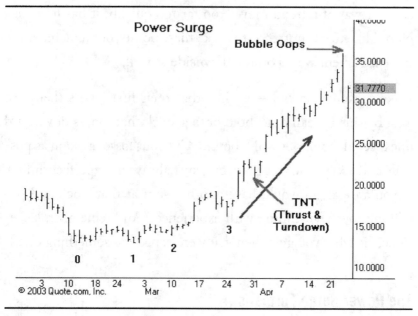

January 29, 2003 thru April 24, 2003
For larger view, go to www.traderslibrary.com/TLEcorner

tops. Note that after the gap, the price peaks out exactly 14 days later (a multiple of 7).

Bubble Oops

At this point, I note a bubble oops, which is the peak of an overly enthusiastic power surge, invariably followed by a quick and strong movement in the opposite direction.

FIGURE 7.5 - HITK—Hi-Tech Pharmacal Co. Inc.—10-minute

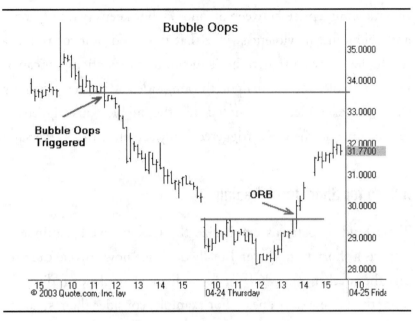

April 23 & 24, 2003

You get a better view of the bubble oops and its resulting movement by going, once again, to the 10-minute chart (figure 7.5).

> **Bubble oops** is a peak price day following a strong trend, followed immediately by correcting movement in the opposite direction.

You see I have noted the prior support level to indicate that the bubble oops triggered an opening range breakdown. This continued strongly until a downward gap formed. But the very next day, the stock turned around again with an opening range breakout. This pattern seems almost to imply that the stock is meant to trade in the mid-range price between 30 and 33, but keeps gyrating above and below in this violent swing. That is a good hint for you as a day trader or swing trader; this is the kind of formation that can be very profitable, one moment on the long side and the next by going short. For example, I have noted that the bubble oops triggered a sell set-up; and the ORB triggered a buy set-up with its reversal.

A Case for Short-term Trading

These kind of patterns emphasize the reason that I continue to work as a short-term trader. I really don't see how anyone can predict the market as a whole or for individual stocks or indices for more than a few days ahead. For example, consider the fast action for PACCAR Inc., as shown on its daily chart (figure 7.6).

This pattern shows you a flat-top breakout, which corresponds to the rule of 4 breakout pattern. But what is really interesting here is the movement of the 50-day moving average. It acts almost like a line of support to the trading range. Then the price moves to a false undercut, which you will recall anticipates a strong move in the opposite direction. It goes beneath the 50 DMA, another strong sign it will correct itself. Then we find a strong gap-'n-go, giving us even more confirming news. This stock is moving upward. So here you have a classic thrust, pause, pivot, NR7, and the rule of 4 breakout. All of these signals converge at the same time.

FIGURE 7.6 · PCAR—PACCAR Inc.—Daily

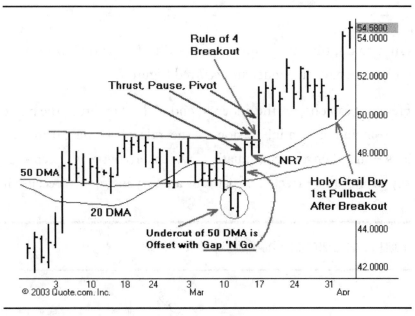

January 28, 2003 thru April 3, 2003
For larger view, go to www.traderslibrary.com/TLEcorner

The Holy Grail

Now, as the price continues upward, you do see a small retreat, but then you come to what well-known trader Linda Raschke calls the Holy Grail formation. This is much like the boomerang because, in this case, it represents the end of the first pullback after the rule of 4 breakout; but, notice how strongly the price takes off right away. There's only a small gap, but a large "go," the kind of pattern every serious investor seeks. This is, indeed, the Holy Grail of price patterns.

> **Holy Grail** a pullback following a breakout, preceding exceptionally strong resumption of price in the trend direction.

Once again, the 10-minute chart provides a micro view of what took place once the undercut occurred (figure 7.7).

Here you can observe the undercut end with a big thrust, the pause day—including a mini-version of the rule of 4 over 10-minute bars—and then the continuation, which of course is exceptionally strong. These fractals of patterns are very instructive because it

FIGURE 7.7 - PCAR–PACCAR Inc.–10-minute

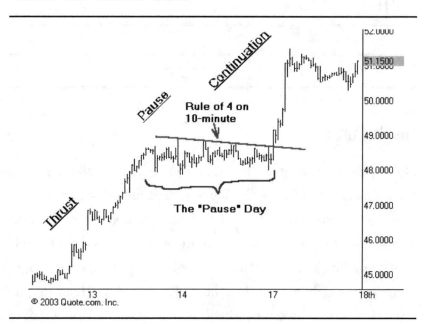

March 12, 2003 midday thru March 17, 2003
For larger view, go to www.traderslibrary.com/TLEcorner

demonstrates how these patterns do play out on every scale. They are predictable and consistent.

Combining Patterns and Signals: Making Them Work for You

I will conclude with one last chart, which shows you how to put patterns and signals together. The daily chart for Quest Diagnostics is interesting in how it reveals the stock's trends (figure 7.8).

Here you see a lot of action taking place beneath the 50-day moving average. When you see an extended play such as this—below

FIGURE 7.8 - DGX—Quest Diagnostics—Daily.

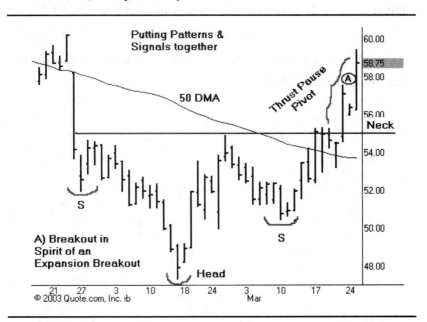

January 16, 2003 thru March 25, 2003

the average—you know the price has to eventually bounce back. A lot comes together here. The inverted head and shoulders signals to you that price is about to correct itself. And sure enough, right after the last shoulder, price takes only three days to move above and to then break through resistance. The head and shoulders patterns predicts this very move, and the set-up occurs and is confirmed when it goes up through the 50 DMA. The move also forms up as a thrust, pause, pivot and then, at A, you see what I think is clearly an expansion breakout. This stock is on the move.

In any and all trading activity, you have to seek the combination of patterns and signals to time your decisions, cut losses, and recognize the set-up as it emerges. If you wait to see whether or not you were right, you lose the opportunity. You won't get to 100%, but why settle for 50% when you can find your range somewhere in between? And if you can use patterns and signals to improve your odds, the profits will follow.

Self-test questions

1. A grenade is:

   a. Any incident occurring on the floor of an exchange that threatens the security of trading or the files and records of the market.

   b. Unexpected bad news about a company, leading to a panic and a large price decline in the stock.

   c. A sudden price move below support or above resistance, that blows up the established trend line.

   d. An officer responsible for security in the exchanges.

2. The bleedback is a formation in which:

   a. Price levels return to previously established trading ranges following a price surge above or below.

   b. The loss of profits experienced by investors through excessive commissions or the taking of small losses to avoid larger ones.

   c. Loss of profitability in trading due to inflation, or from holding onto under-performing stock for too long.

   d. Unexpected profits resulting from mergers or stock splits.

3. The expansion volume breakout is:

   a. The pattern emerging when corporations expand their base of operations.
   b. The combination of a price breakout and unusually high trading volume on the same day.
   c. A trading aberration caused by unusually high activity on the part of institutions, usually occurring at or immediately before the end of the fiscal quarter.
   d. A breakout taking place after a widening trading range was seen.

4. A boomer refers to:

   a. A pattern of two inside bars inside a breakout, or a large range bar followed by a gap-'n-go.
   b. A market maker or specialist whose age corresponds to the baby boomer generation, referred to by younger traders in a derisive manner.
   c. A bar accompanied by exploding volume.
   d. A price gush to the downside, creating widespread panic and a sell-off.

5. The power surge is:

   a. Chronically dangerous to the exchanges, where loss of power could create problems in the orderly trading system.

   b. A reference to manipulative actions taken by institutions to control the price of stocks so they can buy or sell at favorable price levels.

   c. The predictable short-term swings in price that day and swing traders recognize and use to generate fast profits.

   d. A strong price momentum in one direction with little or no pause or swing.

For answers, go to www.traderslibrary.com/TLEcorner

Trading Resource Guide

RECOMMENDED READING

SEVEN SET-UPS THAT CONSISTENTLY MAKE MONEY
by Jeff Cooper

A reliable trading set-up can be worth a fortune in winning trades. In this new DVD course, Jeff Cooper, author of the bestselling Hit and Run books, hands over his seven most consistently profitable set-ups. With great detail, this course provides an explanation of each set-up and examples of the money making power in action.

You won't get any hypothetical theory in this course, just real set-ups from a real trader that will position you to make real money—again and again. Plus, Cooper walks you through his approach to using moving averages that has allowed him to make his living trading.

This collection of tactics balances the homerun big gain set-ups with the consistent, reliable set-ups to give you options that will work in a wide variety of market conditions. These proven technical patterns and powerful understanding of market behavior are ready to work for you.

Item #BCJCx5197574 - $129.00

HIT AND RUN TRADING: THE SHORT-TERM STOCK TRADERS' BIBLE - UPDATED

by Jeff Cooper

Discover winning methods for daytrading and swing trading from the man who wrote the bible on short-term trading. Professional stock trader Jeff Cooper first released his original Hit & Run Trading Book almost a decade ago, taking the short-term trading world by storm. Now, he's back with a newly updated Hit & Run Trading Volume I. Jammed packed with a full arsenal of new tools and strategies to help day traders compete and survive in this fast-paced, volatile arena.

Item #BCJCx3156887 - $100.00

HIT AND RUN TRADING II: CAPTURING EXPLOSIVE SHORT-TERM MOVES IN STOCKS - UPDATED

by Jeff Cooper

With or without Volume I, you'll find plenty of new, high-profit potential strategies and methods in Jeff Cooper's newly updated Hit and Run Trading II. Broken up into 4 main sections highlighting 16 invaluable trading strategies, this updated version is a must for serious traders looking to take their trading and their returns to the next level. Can you profit from Hit & Run II without having read Volume I? Absolutely! Start making money today using Cooper's newest techniques and easy-to-master setups in this recently updated edition.

Item #BCJCx3156889 - $100.00

GANN SIMPLIFIED
by Cliff Droke

While Gann and his groundbreaking investment theories remain enormously popular and applicable today, very few books have been written that explain his concepts in simple, easy to follow and implement language. Now, this hands-on manual helps new and experienced traders alike discover how to apply his winning concepts to their own investing success. You'll find: * The basic foundations of Gann theory * The type of chart Gann felt was the most important - and why * Gann's special swing charting approach * Gann's 24 Never Failing Trading Rules * How he explains support and resistance Plus so much more, when you put the "simplified" teachings of this renowned guru to work for you.

Item #BCJCx17313 - $29.95

UNLOCKING THE PROFITS OF THE NEW SWING CHART METHOD

by Jeff Cooper; Dave Reif Cmt

8-DVD bound set with 302-page manual

The power of this revolutionary method unfolds in over 300 full-color charts. The methods are the result of years of trading, untold lessons from the market and countless hours of studying by Cooper and Reif. What's equally as extraordinary as the systems is the very rare talent that these men possess to convey concepts that are this complex and incredibly effective in a way that is understandable and immediately applicable. Follow along as the strategy is applied to the entire history of the Dow from the 20s till today. Dave's direct enthusiasm and Jeff's wit and confidence are only strengthened by the definitions and explanations provided in the complete preface and appendix. You get every piece needed to implement The New Swing Chart Method.

Get the most understandable explanation of Gann's Square of Nine theory we've ever seen presented. You'll carry that theory into practice as Cooper and Reif detail their personal trading secrets designed to forecast prices and easily see the tops and bottoms before they happen.

Item #BCJCx4212315 - $2,500.00

Free 2 Week Trial Offer for U.S. Residents From Investor's Business Daily:

I NVESTOR'S BUSINESS DAILY will provide you with the facts, figures, and objective news analysis you need to succeed.

Investor's Business Daily is formatted for a quick and concise read to help you make informed and profitable decisions.

This book, along with other books, is available at discounts that make it realistic to provide it as a gift to your customers, clients, and staff. For more information on these long lasting, cost effective premiums, please call us at (800) 272-2855 or you may email us at sales@traderslibrary.com.